FOX SEA

GUIDE TO MODERN SEA ANGLING

10 9 8 7 6 5 4

First published in 2007 by Fox International Group Ltd

This edition published in 2011 by Ebury Press, an imprint of Ebury Publishing

A Random House Group Company

The Random House Group Limited Reg. No. 954009

Addresses for companies within the Random House Group can be found at www.randomhouse.co.uk

A CIP catalogue record for this book is available from the British Library

Penguin Random House is committed to a sustainable future for our business, our readers and our planet. This book is made from Forest Stewardship Council® certified paper.

MIX
Paper from
responsible sources
FSC® C018179

To buy books by your favourite authors and register for offers visit www.randomhouse.co.uk

Printed and bound in India by Replika Press Pvt. Ltd.

ISBN 9780091940270

CONTENTS

This book has the wrong title. It should be the Wily Old Foxes Guide to Sea Angling! For it is written by one of the craftiest and cleverest sea anglers you are ever likely to meet along the shore. Alan Yates, who has stood his corner on the international circuit fishing for the England squad, has become a living legend in sea fishing circles, and while you certainly wouldn't want to be drawn anywhere near him in a match, he is one of those forward thinking anglers who never lets the beach stay still under his feet for long. And while he draws on a fabulous fountain of knowledge, he's always looking forward for ways to catch more fish and develop improved fishing techniques and tackle.

That's why this book is a winner, for it draws on the Folkestone, Kent angler's fantastic knowledge linked with today's trends of modern equipment, lighter rigs and longer rods to get the very best from our changing seas.

I have known and fished with Alan for more years than I care to remember and one thing has always struck me - his total professionalism and dedication to the sport. While some anglers keep it all close to their chest, Alan is always willing to spill the beans so that other people can share in the joys of being by the sea and catching fish from it. You could say that Alan is a natural, a man who fishes by instinct. He is certainly a hunter, during a match he is deadly, freelancing he's just as focussed. Like I said, he's a wily fox who works out the odds in his favour so that he catches fish, and lots of them.

Alan wants you to be a winner too. So the thousands of words of advice, tips and suggestions that follow are based on experience, his successes and sometimes disappointments.

Fox originally wanted Alan to write a book covering the whole sea fishing scene, but like the true trooper he is, he said 'no'. He suggested a fully comprehensive shore angling book, followed by one on boat angling. You see, that's Alan all over. He wanted to empty his head of everything he knows about sea angling and he knew he wouldn't be able to get it between these covers.

My advice is to read this book very carefully, then read it again. The words of wisdom are priceless and if you absorb just 50 per cent of what Alan says I will guarantee your catches will increase.

Alan has one golden rule though; you can't catch fish that aren't there so if you want to be successful pick the right venue, pick the right time of the year and fish the right tide.

Read this book, and follow Alan's rules, and you are bound to be a winner!

Mel Russ

Mel Russ. Editor,
Sea Angler magazine

I hope this book will help sea anglers adapt and cope with the changing face of sea angling. We have gone through some big changes in recent times with the effects of over commercial fishing starting to come home to roost in many regions of the UK. Sea angling is no longer as productive as it was in my youth, although I will add that it was never easy. Nowadays anglers have the distractions of the much easier coarse and game fishing where fish filled puddles produce a fish a cast. However, for those who like a challenge the sea remains vast, wild and natural. No tiny stock ponds, sucker fish or plastic environments. At sea it is raw, rugged and tough going and you need to think on your feet. Hopefully the contents of this book will point you in the right direction and prompt you to make that little bit more effort to make a catch.

I believe the biggest enemy of UK shore anglers is negativity. Some lack the commitment that sea angling requires and it's a national disease to expect the world and when things don't go your way to blame someone else! I seriously do not believe that sea angling is as bad as a few would have you believe and in fact in certain regions of coast and for some species the fishing is better than in the past. The following pages are intended not only as a guide to tackle, techniques etc, but as incentive to go out and try some new ideas. You only have to look at the pages of the angling magazines to see a procession of huge fish being landed throughout the year and hopefully that could be you soon!

The number of sea anglers continues to rise with the summer mackerel, smoothhound, ray and bass seasons replacing the traditional cod season. It's not all doom and gloom and in many regions shore angling is on the up.

There is talk of a national rod licence for sea anglers and that may yet give us a voice in the management of the sea fishery with eventual protection for species like bass and tope as sporting only. A golden mile of inshore coast with commercial fishing banned, more conservation minded commercial minimum fish sizes and "take" limits on fish and bait. Anglers may have to bite the bullet to ensure that sea angling not only survives, but returns to the glory days of the near past!

Tight Lines!

Alan Yates

GET YOUR FISHING FIX EVERY MONTH

SeaAngler

Mel Russ, the editor of Sea Angler magazine, says: "If you really enjoy your sea fishing then I recommend you take out a subscription. Then you will get the nation's favourite sea angling magazine through your letterbox regularly throughout the year...and collect a great tackle gift into the bargain."

TOP REASONS FOR TAKING OUT AN ANNUAL SUBSCRIPTION
- Guaranteed delivery by post to your house
- Exciting gift opportunities
- Expert editorial coverage
- Regular sea angling news
- Big skills section to help you catch
- Advice on catching various species through the seasons
- Exclusive Where to Fish pages
- Big tackle section spotlighting the latest gear
- Specific in-depth tests on rods, reels and boats
- Fabulous angling stories to get you fishing

Easy ways to order
1 Click online: www.gofishing.co.uk/subscribe
2 Call the telephone hot number now 0845 601 1356. Lines open 8.30am-9pm Mon to Fri, 10am-4pm Sat

CHAPTER 1
MODERN TACKLE

There have been some revolutionary advances in sea angling tackle over the last few decades. The arrival of space-age fibres and metals, as well as the micro chip, has greatly improved the manufacture and design of fishing gear. But the biggest advance in tackle has been prompted by the sea itself. Concentrated commercial pressure has depleted many fish species worldwide, while their demise has allowed other less commercially attractive fishes to thrive.

With fewer predators, an untapped food source becomes available. This is being taken advantage of by other species.

UK sea anglers no longer have a year dominated by winter species like cod, and while some see this as a decline, others view it as an opportunity. Other species have become major targets, forcing the angler to consider a different approach to his fishing and his tackle. Match anglers across Europe adapted the quickest simply because they

Target the species around, rather than what your mind dreams of.

Global warming may be the reason given for the arrival of many new species, but Mother Nature's enormous capacity to cope with environmental changes caused by man is a more likely reason.

found it easier, in many cases, to lower their sights or change tactics in order to catch. Now freelance anglers are also taking advantage of the new seasonal species fluctuations when they show, and switching to the common, mundane or smaller fish when they don't. It's not all good news, though. The downside is that some of the big predators of the past are rare, while the most successful species are those that can spawn within a few years, or those that are not commercially valuable, or else are very labour-intensive to market.

However, if anglers move venues and remain alert to the changing seasons and fish migration, the UK's sea angling year is far more prolonged and intricate in many regions than it once was.

Nowadays a single rod and reel cannot cope with this kind of fishing as more and more sea anglers adapt to the changes the sea and its species have forced upon us. If you haven't joined them, then look long and hard at your methods and results – they can be vastly improved by making the most of what's available, rather than staying with the single tactic fishing of the past!

Modern tackle is changing, with more refinement and finesse. Lighter materials have pushed rod lengths out to 16ft-plus and this has greatly increased the casting range of the average sea angler.

Customising of sea tackle is the current boom, with more and more tackle companies like Fox taking sea tackle to another level. If you want to you can still keep your hooks in an old tobacco tin and your tackle in a wicker basket, but most welcome the attention sea angling is getting in terms of tackle specifically designed for the task in hand.

"Modern rods are now custom built to suit the venue, species, season and the angler"

There is a large range of rods suitable for fishing from the shore. Beachcasters fall into two basic categories: rods for use with a multiplier reel and those for use with a fixed-spool reel. Both types have rings which guide the line along the blank to cope with the way each different rod bends and the reel being used.

"Rods with multiplier reels require closely spaced rings"

MULTIPLIER ROD - REEL POSITIONED ON TOP OF ROD

FIXED-SPOOL ROD - REEL POSITIONED UNDER ROD

"Fewer rings are needed on rods for fixed-spool reels"

The multiplier reel is used on top of the rod, with the spool and rod rings facing upwards. Rings are closely spaced and small enough to guide the line along the contour of the rod when it bends, preventing it from touching the blank.

The fixed-spool reel is fixed below the rod with the rings downwards. It requires fewer rings to allow the line to follow the contours of the rod when it bends.

Fox rods come with adjustable reel seats, with the option of a trigger for use with a multiplier.

Fixed-spool rings generally have a larger diameter spool because the line comes off the front of the reel in loops when cast. Larger rings near the reel help pass these loops through the remaining rings smoothly.

To recap, a fixed-spool beachcaster generally has fewer, but bigger rings and a multiplier smaller, but more frequent, rod rings.

It is possible to use a fixed-spool reel on a multiplier rod, but not the other way round, because then the fewer rings will allow the line to cross the blank when it bends. This can cause problems because a loop of line can easily catch around a rod ring during the cast and cause a breakage. Alternatively, the line can rub on the rod or ring leg and be damaged. Either way, it's not worth the risk.

There are also big differences between the action of rods designed for multiplier reels and those for fixed-spool reels. Most multiplier rods have a very stiff butt section with much of the action in the last three feet of the tip. This design is aimed at power casting styles like the pendulum, where power is increased by swinging the lead in a wide arc to lend compression to the rod. Fixed-spool rods, on the other hand, are designed for overhead and off the ground casting styles, where the lead is cast from a standing start. They have more of a through (or softer) action. Multiplier rods have an M in their model or catalogue number and fixed-spool rods the letters F/S.

"Large diameter rings are more essential for use with fixed spool reels"

FIXED SPOOL ROD - EYES POINTING DOWN

MULTIPLIER ROD - EYES POINTING UP

"Rods for rough ground need to be stiffer to help bully fish through kelp and rocks"

An increasing number of beach anglers have adopted the long rod and fixed-spool reel system used by the Continental angler. This allows a more refined approach to sea angling, with the softer rods and lighter main line aimed primarily at smaller fish. Gradually these methods have filtered into UK match fishing and from there into general use, an important factor in their favour being that they promote more success and enjoyment from smaller fish.

The long rod revolution is making sea angling more fun, and is moving the UK style away from its previous "totally casting" ideology. Anglers have found that the species that responded to long range casting in the past, especially cod, are far more scarce. Other fish are now taking their place in the shore angling pecking order and these often involve more thought to catch than the lugworm blasting tactics of the past.

Of course, as with all new ideas nothing is the beginning and end of everything, and basic UK beachcasting tactics still have a place at many times of year and from many venues. Long-range casting has also benefited from the long rod, with multiplier users also finding big distances easier to attain from a standing start and a simpler casting style.

But just like their freshwater cousins, UK sea anglers are realising that being versatile is a way to compensate for deteriorating sport, or to cope with new tactics and individual species or venues. In the past, one rod or style caught everything because there were simply a lot more fish, especially big ones. Nowadays, to be successful, sea anglers need to consider a range of different tactics and gear throughout their angling year.

"The long rod revolution is making sea angling more fun"

Top Tip – One of the biggest advantages of modern long rods is that they are in three sections, and this means that the overall length of the dismantled rod is far less than the old two-piece – great for transporting by car or plane!

A bonus of the longer rods when used with a fixed-spool reel is that casting further is made easier. Lighter, stronger carbon has sent rod lengths soaring, and a longer rod is simply a longer lever which will produce greater average casting distances from a standing start than the heavier, shorter rods of the past. Power and timing are less important, while potential distance from a straightforward overhead thump, even for a novice, is pretty incredible!

The old-time casting gurus can crow all they like, but their techniques are fast becoming redundant, rather like the mountain bike superseding the penny farthing!

But nothing stands still and the long rod revolution has only just begun, because angling minds out there are discovering many other advantages that the long rod can bring. For starters, braided line has been an innovation in UK boat angling circles in recent times with improved bite indication, less resistance to tides because of its lack of stretch and low diameter for its breaking strain.

The problem on the shore is that braid doesn't perform well on the popular multiplier reel because it digs into its own coils, making casting hazardous should the coils trap the line mid cast! But on a fixed-spool reel, braid is a very different proposition.

Not only does it cast smoothly, it offers a smaller surface area per breaking strain than mono against strong tide. It allows lighter leads to be used and, importantly, bite indication is incredible – braid's zero stretch shows the same movement on the rod tip as takes place at the hook!

Braid has a far lower diameter than monofilament per breaking strain, and the difference is so dramatic that sea anglers often change to braid of the same diameter they chose for mono. This is a mistake – switch to the same breaking strain, or slightly heavier than the mono

Fox produce a wide range of braid suited to sea angling.

you previously used. Braid is so tough and strong you can drop the diameter considerably without losing strength against the mono you had on your reel.

The long rod revolution continues in the UK, and the increasing popularity of braid line is bringing even more advances to the system's tackle. Because braid has zero stretch, rods need to be softer to cushion a fighting fish. A mono leader also acts as a safety valve, but essentially it's the rod's length that is the cushion. This has prompted an increasing range of sea quiver tips for both boat and shore. These give the angler the choice of a range of tip sections to suit the lead, the casting distance required and the sea conditions.

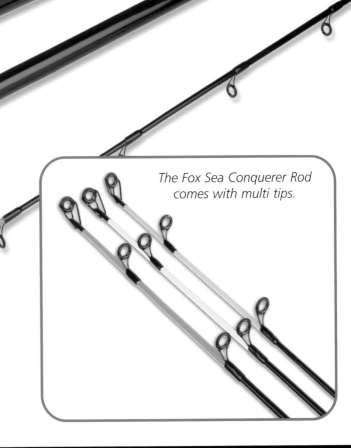

The Fox Sea Conquerer Rod comes with multi tips.

There are two choices of reel position on the rod – high or low. The high multiplier reel position is most suited to rods of 12ft, and the low reel to longer rods up to 15ft. Fixed-spools are generally used in the high position. It is possible to cast with them low, but this is more difficult to master. Many modern beachcasters now include an adjustable tubular reel seat which the angler can fix where he wishes on the rod butt. A point to remember when choosing a new rod is that a fixed reel seat will not allow you to move the reel position to where you wish, even while you are fishing.

Low reel

For the low reel position place the reel at the extreme bottom of the rod butt and then adjust the length of the reducer that slots into the butt to determine the most comfortable position to reel in. If your rod does not have a reducer, place the reel around 10 inches from the butt.

This means that when you reel in with the butt on your hip, the reel will be in a comfortable position to retrieve.

The low reel position can be particularly destructive to reels because it puts them closer to the beach, concrete etc. It's a good idea to take this into account when deciding the length of a rod butt extension (reducer) or fixing a reel seat to a rod butt. Above eight inches, the reel is relatively safe from harm.

Favoured mainly for the multiplier and rods over 13ft, the low reel position is more user-friendly simply because the casting arc of the lead in relation to the angler is larger, and therefore slower and easier to control. The low reel also offers more power to the right arm and better control over large fish, and is more efficient over rough ground.

Most new Fox sea rods come with adjustable reel seats. This allows the reel to be used in any position the angler requires.

Top Tip – This is an excellent way to hold a multiplier reel. It gives you complete control and allows you to feed line.

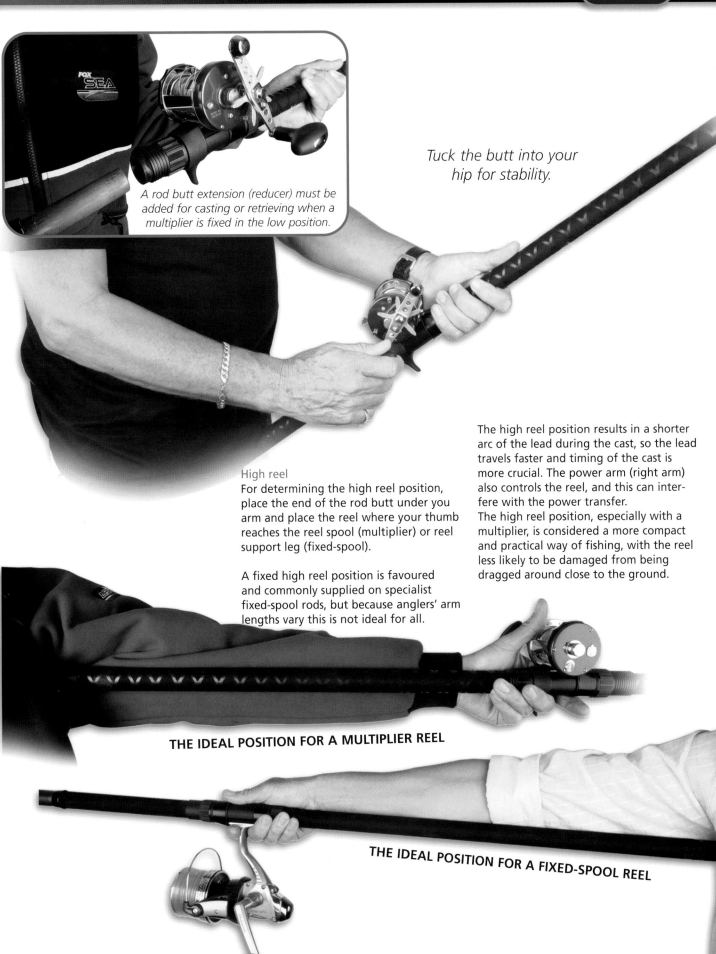

A rod butt extension (reducer) must be added for casting or retrieving when a multiplier is fixed in the low position.

Tuck the butt into your hip for stability.

High reel

For determining the high reel position, place the end of the rod butt under you arm and place the reel where your thumb reaches the reel spool (multiplier) or reel support leg (fixed-spool).

A fixed high reel position is favoured and commonly supplied on specialist fixed-spool rods, but because anglers' arm lengths vary this is not ideal for all.

The high reel position results in a shorter arc of the lead during the cast, so the lead travels faster and timing of the cast is more crucial. The power arm (right arm) also controls the reel, and this can interfere with the power transfer.

The high reel position, especially with a multiplier, is considered a more compact and practical way of fishing, with the reel less likely to be damaged from being dragged around close to the ground.

THE IDEAL POSITION FOR A MULTIPLIER REEL

THE IDEAL POSITION FOR A FIXED-SPOOL REEL

Beachcasters are all marked with their casting rating. You will find this on the butt, usually just up from the reel fitting. This is the amount of lead weight the rod is most suited to cast, or the range it can handle safely. A few beachcasters are rated to cast between 2oz and 8oz, while the majority slot into a narrower rating, These are as follows: 1oz to 3oz for spinning, plugging and float fishing; 2oz to 4oz for estuary or surf bass fishing; 4oz to 6oz for general all-round shore fishing, and 6oz to 7/8oz for rough ground and heavy weather conditions.

It is important to realise that buying just one rod is always a compromise in terms of its casting rating. No single rod can be suitable for all the weights, line breaking strains and types of fishing mentioned.

ROD RINGS
In general the more you pay, the better quality the rod and its fittings. There are lots of functional, economical rods available and also some expensive top of the range models. Look out for quality lined rod rings – these are least likely to break or crack if the rod is dropped.

The legs and feet used to secure rod rings to the rod via cotton whipping can stiffen the rod's action. In the case of the tip section of the lightest rods, single-leg rings are often used to allow the tip to bend more freely. At the stiffer butt end three-leg rod rings are used for strength, and they may be double whipped where close to a joint for extra strength.

Most beachcasters have a coloured tip section to aid bite detection, especially after dark.

Fox has added a spiral of reflective tape to its beachcaster tips to make them stand out in daylight or darkness.

Single leg

Tip and butt rings.

Triple leg

Fox sea rods all come with their own ratings.

MATRIX SURF ELITE 16'

16' CASTING WEIGHT **4-7** oz

16' CASTING WEIGHT **4-7** oz FOX

"High-visibility tips offer instant bite detection day or night"

Top Tip – Low profile or "low rider" line guides are finding increasing popularity on modern beachcasters because they can cope with both monofilament lines and braid lines. Large rings are generally required for monofilament when it is cast using a fixed-spool reel because of the large loops coming off the spool. Braid lines and the latest, more supple copolymer lines do not unload in such large loops and so smaller rings can be used. Braid lines, however, can only be used on a fixed-spool reel. Smaller, low-profile rings produce smoother casting because there is less resistance to the rod through the air and greater stability on the rod rest in strong wind.

Modern rods are made from carbon fibre, and this is a conductor of electricity – beware when fishing near overhead cables of the dangers of touching an electric wire with a carbon rod tip!

REEL SEATS AND GRIPS

Most fixed-spool rods have a fixed screw-up reel fixing called a tubular reel seat or fitting. This means the reel can only be used in the one position. Increasingly common are the latest adjustable, sliding reel seats (Fox Slide Lok) which lock in position when you tighten the reel. These are the most practical because you can decide the reel position to suit you.

Old-style coaster pipe grips are not efficient for many reels, especially the larger capacity models. Adjustable reel seats with a trigger grip are meant for multiplier reels only. Hand grips (EVA) on rods are often used where a fixed reel seat is fitted. The modern alternative is shrink tube or shrink wrap, which is a tight fitting ribbed or patterned PVC or rubber finish that offers an excellent grip in all weathers.

Some Fox sea rods come with both multiplier & fixed-spool reel seats.

ROD JOINTS (spigots)

Several different types of rod joint are used – a simple push-in joint cuts weight and is popular for the longest rods. A spigot joint which allows the two sections to have a level fit is the alternative design. When the tip section is in place in the spigot a small gap is left to allow for wear (this is not a fault, indeed always look for a gap between the joints).

If the joints meet then the tip may be loose fitting. It is common to find a long whipping, sometimes a double whipping, close to spigot joints to add strength. On many of the longest and most flexible rods, like the softer blanks used for fixed-spool reels, simple put-in joints are used to save weight. These are metal banded for extra strength.

Carbon expands when it is warm, and this can cause rod joints to jam. A solution is to cool the male end of the joint down with a freezer block, or even put it under the freezer lid for a few minutes before attempting to pull the joints apart.

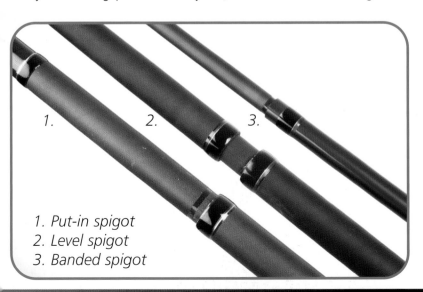

1.
2.
3.

1. Put-in spigot
2. Level spigot
3. Banded spigot

Top Tip – Although light, soft tips in glass and carbon show bites well in a tideless situation and at close range, soft tips bend into strong tides and soak up mono line stretch, making it difficult to see bites at long range. A stiff rod tip is far better for spotting bites at long range.

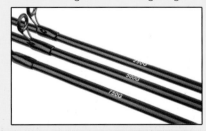

There are two types of reel commonly used for shore fishing – fixed-spool and multiplier. The fixed-spool reel's biggest plus point is that it does not have a revolving spool, therefore line overruns and reel tangles do not occur.

Its performance is far less affected by the angler's skill than that of the multiplier. It's the choice of the novice for this reason, and the fact it can be mastered in seconds. Fixed-spools generally offer a faster retrieve rate than the multiplier because the spool is larger. They are also more suitable for use with low diameter monofilament lines and braid lines, and have a larger working range of line capacity because the spool is wide, rather than deep like that of a multiplier. Fixed-spool reels are easier to cast in confined spaces and from a standing start, while the spool can be changed in seconds, offering the angler the option of spare spools containing different lines, rather than several complete reels. On the downside, the maximum casting range is more difficult to attain than with the multiplier and the reel is considered more cumbersome to use and not as efficient when lifting or cranking heavy weights.

PRICE AND QUALITY

As with all types of tackle the more you pay, the better the product you will get. In the case of a multiplier the more expensive models are superior.

The cheaper fixed-spool models, on the other hand, are often as efficient as the more expensive models. The reason for this is that the fixed-spool system lacks any moving parts that affect the reel's actual casting potential. A cheap fixed-spool has many of the features of one costing far more, and may only lack the spool oscillation slowness and smoothness of a more expensive model. However, a cheap multiplier will lack the vital casting control such as fibre or magnetic brakes and the spool smoothness of ball-bearings, which are standard on the expensive models.

FIXED-SPOOL REELS

Because the fixed-spool reel is also widely used by coarse and game anglers around the world, the variety of models available is huge. They differ in size and line capacity, so a first essential is to choose a model that suits the fishing you intend doing.

Different sized reels are required for beachcasting, estuary fishing, plugging etc, with size based on line capacity. For clear beach angling 12lb to 15lb line is the standard choice, and so a reel that holds a working capacity of around 200/300 yards of 12lb to 15lb line is most suitable.

A majority of the fixed-spool reels suitable for beachcasting are sized via their catalogue number. From 4000 upwards to 7000 or 8000 we have reels suitable for sea angling, but this is not fail-safe, so also check the line capacity, details of which are usually on the spool. The most suitable reels for beachcasting have a profiled or coned spool. Look for a model with a spare spool. This gives you the option of loading the second spool with heavier line for fishing rough ground, or as a back-up spool.

Price is a major factor, and although many of the economy reels will get you fishing, the more expensive models have more refined mechanisms such as smooth ball-bearings and slow oscillating line lays. Bright metallic colours often hide plastic parts and cheap engineering, while quality reels have a far better corrosion-resistance.

For beachcasting your reel will require a front drag – this is the mechanism on the front/top that holds the spool on the reel and allows it to slip and release line under pressure to prevent a pulling fish breaking the line.

Different sized fixed-spool reels.

"The fixed-spool reel is used by freshwater and sea anglers around the world, hence the selection is huge"

For beachcasting the spool needs to be clamped hard down, and only reels with a front drag adjustment allow this. The popular rear drag used for coarse fishing etc cannot be tightened down sufficiently for distance beachcasting.

Balance is an important factor when choosing a reel. Fixed-spools can be gawky and heavy, especially the large cheap models, and these can upset the balance of your rod. Take your rod along to the tackle shop and look for a compact and low-profile reel that sits on the butt so the complete rod is balanced. Also look for a model with comfortable handles, bearing in mind that the winter beach is cold on the hands. A handle that the palm can grip will be the most comfortable.

LOADING YOUR FIXED-SPOOL REEL

Modern fixed-spool reels suitable for sea angling have a long, profiled spool and a working capacity of around 300 yards of line. No need to fill the reel with yards of backing line to fill it up, as was the case with the older, deep spool designs. The modern spool is also contoured to unload the line very efficiently during the cast. It tapers towards the top of the spool.

The line diameter you use will affect the way the reel unloads the line. Thicker line will decrease the diameter of the spool quickly, causing the spool lip to catch the line as it is cast. With a thin line (0.35mm mono and below) the spool decreases less quickly and line flow is more efficient because it doesn't catch on the spool lip. Fixed-spool reels allow the efficient use of lighter mono lines and braid lines, and it is possible to use very low diameter braids from the shore effectively. You can tie the line to the spool via a simple lasso knot or a three-turn Grinner knot.

Avoid knots in the main line because these will stand proud of the spool and catch loops of line as you cast. You will need to fill the reel with line to the top-most lip of the spool.

Loading a Fixed-Spool Reel

1. The first step to tying a three-turn Grinner knot is to pass the line around the spool.

2. Lay your finger along the loop and pass the tag end around your finger and through the loop three times.

3. Remove your finger and pass the tag end through the loops formed by your finger.

4. Draw the knot slowly together and snip off the tag as close as possible.

5. You need to make sure any loops coming off the spool of line are removed as you transfer it to the reel spool.

For general beachcasting (that's shore fishing from clear beaches, piers, estuaries, etc), main lines in monofilament of 15lb breaking strain (0.35mm diameter) are most suitable. So the priority when choosing

a reel for clear ground is that it has a line capacity of approximately 250 yards to 300 yards of 12lb to 20lb line. For rough ground such as rocky or weedy shores a stronger, therefore thicker, main line is required and the spool needs to hold 200 yards-plus of 25lb to 30lb (0.45mm) line.

You will need to add a casting shock leader. This is a stronger length of line at the front of the main line that takes the shock of casting the lead. Cast a 6oz lead with 15lb main line and it will break off, with potentially disastrous consequences.

Leader strength is determined by multiplying each ounce of the lead's weight by 10lb of breaking strain – for example, 5oz lead/50lb shock leader; 6oz lead/60lb shock leader. Field or competition casters should add another 10lb to be on the safe side.

LEAD	MIN LEADER
4oz x 10lb	40lb
5oz x 10lb	50lb
6oz x 10lb	60lb
7oz x 10lb	70lb
Powercaster or Tournament add 10lb. Check regularly for damage.	

OSCILLATING LANE LAY

This important device moves the bale arm up and down the spool as it rotates around it and lays the line on the spool evenly. The more expensive models have a more intricate oscillating line lay system which loads the line slowly and evenly, cotton reel fashion, and this increases spool capacity and improves casting smoothness. Some cheap reels with a poor line lay and deep spools bulge the line unevenly on the spool, or the spools churn and rock as they are retrieved. These should be avoided.

An even line lay will aid casting.

REEL ADJUSTMENT, SETTINGS AND FEATURES

Of particular advantage to the sea angler is the anti backwind mechanism (below). This is a small lever, generally positioned underneath or at the rear of most models.

Flip this and the handle will reverse – a really effective way to release line should a big fish threaten to break you. Bearing in mind the drag is clamped shut, in an emergency you can always back wind!

A roller bearing in the bale arm acts as an anti twist device, allowing the line to run smoothly at right angles to the spool. On cheaper models this can stick or wear, a point worth checking because a good roller bearing will prolong line life.

Most spools have a line clip on the side of the spool to clamp the end of the reel line when not in use. Fixed-spool reels have an annoying habit of expelling loops of shock leader line, and this clip solves the problem. An elastic band or Velcro rod band also serves to prevent the line from unravelling. The line clip can also be used to set casting distance by clipping up the line at the distance required so that consecutive casts will reach the same spot – something you cannot do with a multiplier.

The retrieve ratio of the reel (5.3 to 1, 6 to 1 etc) relates to the number of turns of line laid around the spool for each turn of the handle. Fixed-spools have a faster line retrieve than multipliers because the spool is bigger, and the line diameter on the spool does not decrease by much.

All models include an automatic bale arm return. On some this is simply a bumper the bale arm hits to flip it back into position – on the more sophisticated models the return is internal and far smoother. A majority of fixed-spool reels are ambidextrous and can be swapped from left to right-hand wind in seconds, a big plus for left-handers because they can buy a top class fixed-spool reel, whereas if they want a multiplier they have only a couple of inferior left-hand models to choose from.

TIPS - FIXED SPOOL REELS

- Tapered shock leaders are ideal for the fixed-spool because the smaller leader knot is less prone to catch loops of line on the spool or the caster's finger.

- A finger stall, glove or casting trigger greatly assists casting and protects the user.

- Many of the cheaper front drag models, once clamped down tight for casting, are not easy to loosen and this is another reason why the more expensive models are more efficient – their front drags have a click mechanism to prevent jamming and they can be released quickly should a fish threaten to break the line.

- Big pit fixed-spool reels designed for carp fishing are also ideal for very long-range sea angling.

- You have threaded the line through your rod rings and then find the line is outside the bale arm. No panic, simply unscrew the front drag, remove the spool, open the bale arm and then replace the spool.

- The fixed-spool requires far less maintenance than the multiplier because there are fewer moving parts to affect performance. Wash the reel in soapy water after use, rinse and allow it to dry in the air. Lubricate via the oil ports.

An old toothbrush is the ideal tool to get at the dirt etc around the spool and casing of reels.

"Fixed-spool reels are relatively tangle free and so are the first choice of many beginners"

The multiplier is a popular reel for shore and boat angling in the UK although that's not the case across the rest of Europe where the fixed spool dominates. The multiplier's compactness and cranking retrieve power are more suited to the heavier UK style of angling which involves long casting, bigger fish and rough ground. Some say it transmits a greater feeling of direct contact to the fish. The downside is the reel's potential for an overrun or tangle (the birds nest), although it must be said that the modern versions with magnetic and mechanical fibre brakes plus ball bearings are far less prone to this problem.

However, the line diameter used, the capacity of the spool and how neatly the line is laid on the spool during the retrieve are all crucial to this reel's casting performance and some skill and knowledge are essential.

Quoted spool capacities of multipliers are generally for the maximum amount of line the spool can hold and this is not always the best working capacity. An overloaded multiplier can be difficult to control and is more prone to overrun. Under fill the spool slightly if you are a novice caster. A range of different size multiplier reels are available and buying the correct size reel for your fishing is very important. One reel is not totally suitable for all types of shore fishing or venues. Some manufacturers use a reel sizing system and models between 5000 and 7000 are most suitable for shore angling. The line capacity of the reel gives you a clue to its best use. The small spooled models (6000/65000) with a capacity of approximately 250/300 yards of 15lb (0.35mm) are designed for fishing light line, clean ground and long range casting.

The best of these also feature magnetic and fibre brakes to improve casting and spool control as well as ball bearings to improve smoothness and line flow. The larger model multipliers (7000/75000) designed for rough ground or light boat fishing have a bigger spool capacity of around 200/300 yards of 20lb, or even 30lb line.

There are a few models that sit between these two main sizes and these are the choice of the shore angler wanting one all round reel, although the casting range of such models is dramatically reduced as the line diameter increases and so you will need different models to get the absolute best results for long range casting or rock fishing!

Retrieve ratios differ between models with the higher retrieve rates more suitable for skimming tackle back over rough ground. On average between 5 to 1 and 6 to 1 are preferred.

Pay the most you can afford for a multiplier. Cheap models without magnetic or fibre brakes, or bearings are difficult to control during the cast, especially for beginners. One piece machined spools and frames are also stronger and will withstand the rigours of the marine environment for longer.

A small 5000 multiplier reel.

A medium sized 6000 multiplier reel.

A large (6000/65000/7000) multiplier reel.

Top Tip - Never use a reel with knots in the line, these have the potential to cause an overrun and will snap under pressure or damage your thumb! Braid line does not work efficiently on a multiplier for shore casting.

REELING IN

The simplest way to retrieve when you are fishing is to place the rod butt between your legs when you reel in. This gives you plenty of purchase. If you fish with the multiplier reel low down then you can place the butt on your hip. But don't crank the reel against a heavy weight or snag because this can damage the reel's main pinion gear.

Instead lift the rod dragging the weight in and then reel as you lower the rod. You can also walk back and then reel as you walk forward in extreme situations - this is called pumping and is the way to beat large fish or lumps of weed etc.

Use the palm of your hand to prevent reel rocking when you retrieve.

LOADING YOUR MULTIPLIER REEL

The choice of the line used is very important. Thick line (0.40mm plus) empties from the spool quickly, doesn't cast so far and catches lots more tide.
Too thin line (0.25mm) is prone to overload the spool causing overruns as well as damage or break in the hostile sea environment. If you are a novice caster start with 0.38mm (18lb) monofilament line for the small models and 0.45mm (25lb) for the bigger models. Don't select line by the breaking strain, it's line diameter that matters most, because this effects how the reel spool unloads the line. You can tie the line to the spool
(pic 1) via a simple lasso knot or a three turn Grinner knot, see page 21 for illustration. Reel the line on the spool evenly, cotton reel style, especially for the lower layers. Large knots and uneven bumps and humps transfer through the layers also causing spool vibrations and overruns, so lay line carefully.
You will need to fill the spool with line to its best working capacity and this is normally to within 1cm of the lip. (pic 2) Novice casters are advised to under fill the spool and increase the line load as their casting skills improve and never fill the spool to its stated full capacity. (pic 3)

Spooling a Multiplier.

1. Tie line onto spool.

2. Fill the spool with line.

3. With the spool with line to within 1cm of the lip.

"Lay the line on the spool by guiding it with finger and thumb as you retrieve for cotton reel like line lay"

REEL ADJUSTMENT, SETTINGS AND FEATURES

Most multipliers cast efficiently straight out of the box after loading with line. The lateral movement and smooth flow (float) of the spool can be adjusted via the screw down end caps on the reel's side plates, whilst the brakes, plus magnets are used to adjust the spool's speed when casting. Some reels allow adjustment during the cast via a knob or slide for the magnets.

Fibre or plastic brake blocks are a minimum requirement of a beach casting multiplier, so totally avoid reels without brakes! Most have a minimum of two (some up to six) brake blocks, usually located at the handle end of the spool, and these operate by centrifugal force as the spool spins forcing the brakes outwards on their pins to rub on the spool and slow it down.

Some models are supplied with the brake blocks locked down or lose in the box, check this with your tackle shop and get him to fit or adjust them.

The quality multipliers include an "easy take apart" system involving two or three finger screws.
This allows the handle side plate to be removed to get at the spool, bearings, brakes, etc.

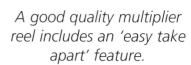

A good quality multiplier reel includes an 'easy take apart' feature.

Mag Multiplier

A lever or slide on the reel back plate allows the magnets to be placed closer to the spool, thus increasing their magnetic force on the metal spool.

Before Cast   **After Cast**

With magnets set full on the spool is slowed dramatically. It's a good idea to put magnets full on first cast when line is dry.

Before Cast   **After Cast**

The magnets still have an effect in the 'off' position and can also be adjusted during the cast to slow reel spool down.

Magnetic brakes on a multiplier reel. They can be removed as required.

Magnetic brakes are the most effective type of casting control for multipliers and they work via the force of a magnetic field affecting the metal spool. Most have upto six magnets and braking adjustment is via a slide or ring on the reel's rear side plate which move the magnets closer or away from the spool.

LEVEL LINE MECHANISM

Some multiplier models have a line lay system which helps the angler to lay the line on the spool evenly, but it restricts casting distance and magnifies casting overrun tangles. My advice is to avoid level lines like the plague! If you must use one choose a tapered shock leader because this allows the use of a smaller, less restrictive leader knot.

Power handles offer several positions via their centre fixing holes and allow the reel handle to be cranked faster to increase the speed of the retrieve.

The star drag is situated below the handle, it is star shaped and is a safety mechanism to prevent a hooked fish breaking the line. Turning the star loosens or tightens the pressure on the spool. If a fish threatens to break the line loosening the star allows the spool to slip and release line via the drag washers.

Spool release button on a multiplier reel. This type automatically re-engages when handle is turned.

Spool release lever on a multiplier reel.

Some multipliers have a ratchet or line out alarm. This can be used for threading the line through the rod rings, or for bite detection.

There are two types of free spool release, the button and the lever. The button release has an automatic re-engage when the handle is turned; the lever has to be physically switched to either position.

Both have their fans with the button release most suspect in terms of water entering the reel mechanism. Some small multipliers have a thumb bar release which is intended for close control when casting lures.

Top Tip - Tapered leaders are a popular way of overcoming a bulky knot between main line and leader and for use with a level line mechanism.

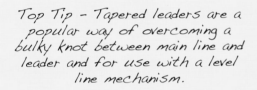

The Star Drag feature on a multiplier reel. Adjustment of star drag is clockwise for on and anti clockwise for off.

Top Tip - Use a genie link or a swivel to help thread line through rod rings.

RODS AND REEL MAINTENANCE AND USE

Having spent a small fortune on a new rod and reel the novice can easily ruin new gear both by misuse and lack of maintenance. The latter is a major problem with buying cheap tackle. Its corrosion resistance and strength may be wanting, especially in the hands of the unskilled or negligent angler.

Modern tackle manufacturing processes and sources ensure that even the most economical tackle has a professional look. Rods have smooth, sometimes fancy whippings and high build gloss finishes with most of the more expensive rod rings and fittings copied. Cheap reels have a metallic look with the aid of plastic metal finishes and the only real guide to quality is to buy the reputable makes, buy the best you can afford and avoid the really cheap rods and reels.

Essential are quality rod rings that will not break if the rod is dropped. We are all clumsy at times and accidents happen. Rods get pulled over by the tide, blown over by wind or dropped on the garage floor and if a ring shatters it can ruin your day.

ASSEMBLING A ROD AND REEL

Spigot joints are made so that there is a gap between the two sections. This is because carbon wears away with friction and if the edges of the joint butted up closely with each other any wear would result in a lose joint and the chance of the tip popping out mid cast. Keeping the spigot clean of sand and grit will extend its life. When assembling, make sure that the spigot or joint is pushed tightly together. A major cause of rod breakages are joints not pushed together, casting then puts pressure on the wall of the rod joint causing it to fracture when the rod is flexed. Make sure the sections fit together snugly and the rod rings are aligned, but avoid tapping the butt against the ground because this can cause the joint to jam. It is important when separating joints not to grip the rod rings, this will cause them to twist and damage: grip the blank close to the joint and twist and pull in a straight line. Fox beachcasters come with a roughened grip area close to either side of the joint which makes joints easier to separate on a cold wet beach.

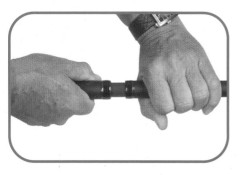

If your rod joint is stuck get the help of another angler and gently twist and pull in a straight line, one on each section.

Most modern beachcasters have an adjustable reel seat, keep these free of sand, the slot that guides the reel clamp can misalign on the cheap models causing it to jam, even over ride the thread, another reason to buy only the best makes like the Fox Slide Lok.

With careful use modern carbon rods are virtually impossible to break, but there are rules that will keep your rod whole and these include never picking a rod up by the tip. Similarly, never flex the rod tip with your hands or try to break out of a snag with the rod tip. You can break any rod by jerking the tip too hard, or placing too much pressure on the tip by hanging a heavy weight vertical. The procedure for pulling for a break is to point the rod tip at the snag, wrap the line above the reel around the butt a couple of times and walking backwards - slowly.

BEATING CORROSION AND MAINTENANCE

The biggest enemy of the sea angler is salt corrosion and even the most expensive tackle will corrode if the gear is left salty wet in a damp atmosphere. It's essential to wash rods and reels with warm soapy water after use and then allow them to dry in the air.

Rod bags are preferred by lots of anglers, but they can be self defeating if the rod is not washed free of salt because they retain a damp salty atmosphere after use. Similarly reel bags enclose reels with the salt they have gathered between trips.

The smallest casting multipliers in particular are delicate machines and they need to be maintained and cleaned regularly. Leave ANY make or model in your tackle box salty for a couple of weeks and it will corrode. Brush off salt, crud, etc with a tooth brush under a warm tap after each trip and allow it to dry in the open air. Oil bearings, spool ends and handle every few months.

Lots of sea anglers like to take reels apart, especially multipliers, in order to get them to run more smoothly and to cast further. In the past the obsession with distance casting ruined many an angler's reel because they took notice of the field casting hype about removing grease or using this or that oil. In recent years advice to remove some of the magnets from reels has further complicated the issue. For general fishing it is not advisable to strip reels of grease or oil, this helps keep the salt water and corrosion at bay. Re-oiling a multiplier reel is not that important in terms of distance, a quality reel with bearings will retain oil for a considerable time and it's only a few of the faster models that are designed for casting a lead alone that need extra attention to oils. Best of the reel oils is Red Rocket Fuel.

Magnetic brakes work superbly straight from the reel's box and the slide adjustment that takes them closer or further away from the spool is adequate. Magnets should not be removed unless you are fully conversant with the reel's working parts and your casting needs. If you do take out the odd magnet then watch out because it is a tricky business on some of the models because once released all the magnets automatically clamp together.

Don't allow your reel to be immersed in sea water, even the best reels will not withstand a swim and then being left for a month in a tackle box. If your reel gets dunked wash it out and allow to dry before returning to the tackle box.

ON THE BEACH REPAIRS

There comes a time when an accident will

occur whilst you are fishing, a broken rod tip ring, a jammed reel seat etc. Be prepared for such eventualities with a small stick of Hot Melt glue and lighter which are easy to use to replace a broken or loose ring. Simply heat a tip ring with the lighter flame to remove it,

remember it will be hot so use pliers, rather than your fingers! Heat the glue and melt into the hole in the spare tip ring and replace, remembering to line it up with the intermediate rings before the glue sets. You can also replace an intermediate ring by cutting back one whipping, pulling the ring out and pushing the new ring leg in the hole left in the remaining whipping. Hot Melt or PVC tape can be used to secure it.

Hot melt

"Buying quality tackle, especially good rod rings helps ensure it stands up to wear and tear of sea angling"

Do you carry a coffin-sized tackle box to the beach or pier that contains all but the kitchen sink. Do you carry lots of unnecessary items, and do you get back pain? If the answer is yes, you are not alone – there are countless sea anglers who cannot leave any item of tackle at home "just in case". Size-wise, a tackle box around 15 x 18 x 15ins is the most compact. Bulk and weight are the angler's enemies, especially when a long walk is involved to reach your venue. You can save on weight by spreading and balancing your load, and a large bucket for bait, the catch etc will help. The other alternative is a tackle trolley. Several custom-made versions suitable for the beach are available.

Most sea angling tackle boxes are nothing more than plastic water cisterns, and boxes have only improved since the wicker

basket in that they are now waterproof! Whatever type of tackle box you own, the carry strap is an important item to discard. Instead, fit a back rest/carry frame to the box. This allows you to carry the box rucksack style, which distributes the weight evenly and does less damage to your back! Other extras include a side tray, cushions and

several custom-made inserts. A few have drawers, and nothing is more infuriating on a wet day than having to dig inside your box to find that what you want is at the bottom of one of these.

Rucksacks are lighter than boxes, and favoured by anglers fishing long distances away from the car. They do, though, allow gear to get wet. A good tip here is to include a plastic tray in the base of your rucksack to help keep it stable and the base dry.

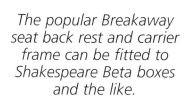

The popular Breakaway seat back rest and carrier frame can be fitted to Shakespeare Beta boxes and the like.

YOUR TACKLE LOAD

The quantity of tackle you own will mount up quickly, and items like lead sinkers can be particularly heavy, so be positive about what you need and don't need for a fishing trip. Take a minimum of 10 leads, including 5oz or 6oz fixed and breakouts (a fixed wire 7oz lead can be handy when the weather is rough). In the winter don't carry floats, lures or small leads that you use only in summer, and have a few breakout leads without wires to cover the plain lead option.

The screw-in heads of the Gemini lead system allows leads to be converted easily.

Terminal rigs have their own chapter later, but a full rig wallet can be essential to the sea angler because it offers a range of options for different venues, weather conditions, species and baits. You can thin out your rig wallet if conditions and venues are known before you go fishing. There's no need to carry winter rigs in summer, or vice-versa.

If you have a full rig wallet, why do you need to carry a giant bits box of terminal accessories and hooks? Slip a small selection of assorted swivels, links, crimps, beads, hooks etc into your rig wallet.

If you do need to carry an accessory box with spare swivels, beads and crimps, also use it to store spare bait cotton, rod rings, hot melt glue, a lighter, booms, baiting needles, etc. The best boxes are the pliable plastic type that won't split when cold. Ensure items in compartments cannot mix if the box is turned upside down, and that the lid is secure.

Some anglers carry up to five multipliers loaded with different line loads and breaking strains, plus a fixed-spool loaded with braid in summer. Spare spools are another way of saving on weight. Rods can be kept compact inside a holdall. The type with clips and pull-tight straps are handy for ease of loading up rods, shelter and rod rest.

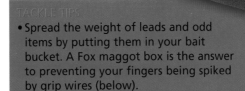

TACKLE TIPS

• Spread the weight of leads and odd items by putting them in your bait bucket. A Fox maggot box is the answer to preventing your fingers being spiked by grip wires (below).

• Add several of the small sachets of anti corrosion granules found in electrical equipment to your box to prevent moisture and corrosion. (Below)

• Shingle can lodge in the carry frame or feet of a box, and mud or sand stick to the bottom. Rod holdalls can fill up with sand and all add weight, so have a regular check.

• Keep a first aid kit in your car and carry a few sticking plasters in your rig wallet.

• A fish measure (below) is essential because lots of species have a legal minimum takeable size.

• A sealable plastic rig bag with a few spare hooks will save weight. If you must carry a whole box of hooks, put these in bags to discourage corrosion.

• Check out the venue and weather conditions before you go to a venue and you may be able to dispense with the reel loaded with heavy line etc, or carry tapered leaders for a quick change, saving on the number of reels you need to carry as spares. Dispensing with heavy reel cases also saves on weight.

The shore-based sea angler simply cannot fish without a rod rest. Holding your beachcaster can be a fun way to fish when the fish are biting regularly, but between bites, especially in cold weather and when baiting up or preparing tackle, it's just not practical to fish without a rest. It keeps your valuable rod and reel out of the sand and away from corrosive salt water, clear of the rough and tumble of a rock face, pier wall or promenade. It allows you to position the rod tip at a comfortable height to spot bites, and comes with an array of custom-made attachments and accessories that make beach fishing that much easier.

The most basic rod rest is the single sand spike monopod, but this is suitable only for beach and sand because it needs to be pushed into the ground to make it stand up. It's a handy rest for your spare rod when fishing moving up the sand in surf. Other advantages of this type is that it is light to carry long distances, and lifts the line high above the breakers.
The downside is that watching bites can give you a stiff neck!

The tripod is by far the most popular rod rest because it is versatile, being suitable for fishing anywhere, even on a concrete promenade or rock mark. It's also the most stable design for fishing in a high wind and rough seas, and will support two rods. Some of the metal tripods are heavier than others and although the rod height is the same and the alloys are similar it's the dimensions of the angular and round legs that vary, adding weight.

Aluminium alloy is prone to discolouring, although generally it stands up to the salt air well. Give your rod rest the occasional wash down in soapy water to remove the crud – otherwise its life span is pretty well indefinite. Metal threads are more prone to corrode and jam than plastic, although plastic-headed metal screws can sometimes break.

TRIPOD ACCESSORIES AND FEATURES
Legs: Most manufacturers use an angled length of aluminium alloy for the main rear leg of the tripod for strength, with tubular front legs for lightness. Average length is 5ft, with the top-of-the-range models having telescopic front legs and, on some of the longer models, an extendable back leg.

Double head and double cup: Most models have adjustable heads and cups into which the rod is placed. These can be moved up and down the back leg, allowing the rod tip to be raised high above the breakers if required.

"A tripod rod rest allows precise positioning of the rod anywhere on mud, sand, beach or promenade"

They also swivel for easy storage. The top rest is usually a V or U shape and the bottom is a cup into which the rod butt sits. Adjuster screws and fittings are generally of brass, alloy or plastic.

Stabilisers and leg bracers: Most of the best rod rests have stabilising bars or leg braces that prevent the tripod legs from splaying out and collapsing. These are essential for concrete promenades, or anywhere the legs might otherwise slip.

Trace bar, trace clips: A variety of clips and trace bars that clip on to the legs are supplied from which to hang spare terminal rigs etc. Some are plastic, others are metal, with several models having bars that give extra stability when clipped between the two front legs.

Bucket hook: A common feature on most tripods is a central bucket hook under the rod rest head. This can be used to hang a bucket containing bait, tackle etc, or – in a high wind – a bag full of stones can be hung on it to help with stability.

Foot lever: This is a folding section of plastic or aluminium on the back leg, used to help drive the rod rest leg into sand or beach.

Leg clips: These secure the tripod legs together for ease of carriage.

Feet: Metal or plastic pointed feet are used on most rests to help dig them in the beach or grip concrete. They are hard on rod holdalls!

Tripod net, work centre, clip-on bait box: An assortment of extras are available for tripods.

"Umbrellas are light and easy to erect and carry long distances, but a Beach Buddy is more spacious and offers better protection in all weathers"

Some form of shelter will be essential for anglers fishing from a fixed position on the beach, and there are a large number of designs to choose from. Where the angler is subject to lots of movement because of the flooding or ebbing tide, a light, compact umbrella is favoured. Any kind of shelter can be invaluable, not only to keep the angler warm and dry, but to shelter his tackle and bait from the worst of the weather. However, on venues with an appreciable difference between the low and high tide marks, good waterproofs may be a more important consideration.
Here are a couple of shelter options to consider.

THE BEACH BUDDY
The Beach Buddy design of shelter (left) is the best there is. Once erected it is a spacious and stable base camp, ideal for match anglers and freelance anglers who prefer fishing from a fixed station on the high tide line. It is quick and easy to erect on the beach because bucketfuls of stones can be piled on to the flaps at its base. Sand can also be used for this task, while from promenades rocks, pebbles or your tackle box or bucket will all help to keep the Beach Buddy anchored down.

UMBRELLAS
All the umbrellas (below) produced for angling are designed primarily for coarse fishing, and most are not entirely suited to the marine environment. However, having said that, with careful use an umbrella can be far more versatile than a custom made angling shelter. The umbrella's biggest plus point is its compactness and weight. Lighter and easier to carry over long distances, and simpler to erect than the shelter, it can be moved easily during a fishing session.

Umbrellas are made in a range of sizes, the largest of these having zip-up sections for a freshwater pole to travel back through, or a flat back. The largest (50in-plus) are mostly unsuitable for the beach because they catch the wind. Chose a 45in umbrella for beach fishing and it will prove both light to carry and easy to erect, even in a stiff breeze. Some umbrellas offer carbon or plastic stays – great to combat corrosion, but not as stable in a strong wind as metal. The best are coated metal stays. A weak point on many brollies is the fabric at the end of the stays, which is prone to splitting.

Some form of tilt system, as well as an extension on the main pole, is essential – it makes more space available inside the umbrella and allows the main pole to be pushed into the beach and anchored by digging out the sand or shingle and piling it on to the brolly fabric or wings.

Brolly wings are a feature of some and these also increase the overall area of shelter that the brolly offers, as well as allowing it to be anchored more securely by piling stones and the like on the wings.

A coarse angling brolly attachment can be added to your tackle box frame to help support your umbrella on concrete, or to take a high-level bait tray (page 93).

"(below) A shelter offers invaluable protection against harsh weather. (left) The Beach Buddy is regarded as the best type of shelter available"

MONOFILAMENT

If you are not a polymer chemist and not totally familiar with the complicated and ever-changing technology, manufacturing process or materials of modern co-polymer fishing lines then you are not alone.

Neither are many of the distributors and tackle firms that sell lines throughout the UK. They buy monofilament lines in bulk from around the world, without really knowing the detailed technical changes that are continually taking place in line manufacture.

Modern monofilament lines are a vast improvement on the original nylon monofilaments that were developed in the 1930s. The first monofilament fishing lines came in two qualities, with the more expensive lines pre-stretched. This process strengthened them and lowered their diameter. Cheaper, standard mono lines were of very mixed quality.

Recent technology has blended and reinforced the polymer matrix of monofilament lines with various combinations of nylon polymer construction, resulting in lines of specific qualities – more strength, less stretch, more abrasion-resistance, easier flow and so on. In the case of sea angling lines, the co-polymer influence is universal and the change in lines from those of 40 years ago is dramatic. Few, if any, of the old-style monofilaments still exist, and even the cheapest of lines now shows the influence of co-polymer technology. Modern lines are tougher, have less memory, less stretch and a more regular diameter, and differ enormously in their specifications. This brings a tremendous level of choice to anglers, and the good news has continued with the arrival of fluorocarbons and other materials, ensuring that fishing line will continue to evolve and improve.

Buy your line by diameter, not breaking strain, because this will have the most influence on its behaviour on the reel spool. Note that lines differ greatly when diameters and breaking strains are compared. Most beachcasting multiplier reels cast their best distances with line diameters within a small range (0.30mm to 0.38mm). Go too thin, or too thick, and the reel cannot unload the line efficiently. This produces overruns or a reduction in the distance cast, and can even influence the retrieve speed of lures – which, in turn, affects catch rates. Very low diameter lines perform best on a fixed-spool reel, but on a multiplier these can cause overruns.

BRAID LINE

The biggest advantage of using braid line is its lack of stretch and lower diameter for a given breaking strain. It has become increasingly popular in sea angling in recent years as sea anglers have discovered its advantages and how to get the best from it. From the shore it can be successful in calm water at medium range, but in a rough sea its lack of stretch sees it pick up sea movement and transfer it to the rod tip. It cannot be used efficiently with a multiplier for beachcasting, and most who have adopted braid for shore casting have done so with a fixed-spool reel.

Braid is popular for spinning and lure fishing because it gives direct contact with a fish taking the lure, while at the same time, if the lure touches a rock, this fact is transmitted to the angler and he can react. One essential is the use of a mono shock leader in many shore fishing situations to provide a cushion against braid's abrupt lack of stretch. Rods for braid are softer, to compensate for this. Look out for a big improvement in braid lines when they are blended with mono – you'll then be able to buy line with a precise degree of stretch!

LINE CARE

Monofilament line is subject to considerable wear and tear, especially the lower diameter monofilaments (under 0.40mm/20lb). Mono will discolour with use, and this is the time to consider replacing it.

Also look out for abrasion, nicks and flattening or twists in the line. Modern co-polymer lines are particularly tough and abrasion-resistant, but it is a false economy to keep a line for too long – it could cost you fish. The larger diameter lines above 0.40mm/20lb are tougher and will last longer on the spool, while braid line is especially tough and resistant to knocks. It will last far longer than mono.

Most anglers find it essential to completely replace line after a number of fishing trips. You can save on costs by buying line on bulk spools (below). Another way to economise is to remove line and reverse it so that the unused section at the bottom of the spool is now at the top.

Never use line with a knot in it, other

than the shock leader knot. Any knots promote line tangles and overruns, are potential weak points, and may damage your finger when you are casting with a multiplier.

Take special care when loading new line on a fixed-spool reel. It's essential to wind the line on the spool so that any loops or twists are removed, or else they will remain and the line will coil as you cast. To remove twists, wind the line off the spool while it revolves, or, if the twists persist, off the front or rear of the spool by holding the line spool by the edges.

Braid lines are particularly hard-wearing and will outlast mono tenfold.

LINE TOP TIPS

- Colouring line, it is claimed, weakens it. However, this is miniscule and has no real effect on line strength in the diameters used for beachcasting. (12lb to 30lb).

- Many clear lines are white or opaque under water. It is claimed that red is the first colour to disappear from the spectrum, 6ft below the sea's surface.

- Knock or impact strength is a vital quality of lines which are to be used in the harshest sea angling environments. Take particular care when selecting a line of low diameter. Thin lines with high breaking strains may sound great, but is their knock strength and abrasion-resistance up to the task? Okay for distance over clear ground, but it may be better to opt for a bigger diameter for rough ground fishing!

- The world's major line manufacturers were Germany, America and Japan, but nowadays line is also made in India and China, among other places. Line is bought and sold in huge bulk by distributors who spool, label and package it for the world market, and few lines reveal their country of origin. Many apparently different makes and labels are in fact the same line.

- Such is the competitive nature of the manufacture of mono line, the quality and technology is high and there are few, if any, dud lines!

- You might favour a line because of its colour. Field casters like bright yellow or orange because potentially hazardous snap-offs can be found easily. Bright colours are also easier to untangle in a crowded angling situation.

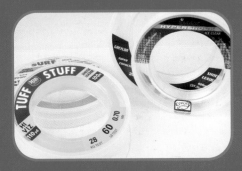

- The breaking strain conversions on spools are not always correct, and for 15lb vary between 6.5kg and 8kg – the actual conversion is 6.8kg.

- The sales pitch? Some line labels make for confusing reading. Just what do laser tested stretch, resin impregnated or polyester lubricated mean? The man on the beach will soon find out what lines are best, and no amount of jargon will decide otherwise.

- Specialist lines are available for hook snoods including some extra tough, low memory co-polymer lines such as Amnesia and Super Snood.

- A Velcro rod band can be used to retain line on the spool. Line clips are often too small for 60lb-plus leader line.

37

GOT THE BOOK...NOW GET SEA ANGLER MAGAZINE

● Alan Yates certainly knows his shore fishing, that is why he is one of the kingpins of Sea Angler, Britain's favourite sea angling monthly magazine.

● But, of course, the subject of saltwater fishing is wide and varied and that is why we have pulled together an expert team to explain how to buy the correct tackle, use the right baits and rigs, cast big distances safely and catch more fish from the sea.

● We also cover areas that others magazines fear to go. Every issue carries guides to the best fishing marks, a comprehensive Where to Fish section, and the massively popular Penn Sea League, which sees the best match anglers in the country going head to head.

● So whether you are dedicated competition angler, specimen hunter, charter or dinghy fisherman, or you just want to idle your time away by the sea, then Sea Angler is just for you.

To get your copy speak to your local newsagent, call our subscriptions line on 0845 6011356 or visit www.gofishing.co.uk/subscribe

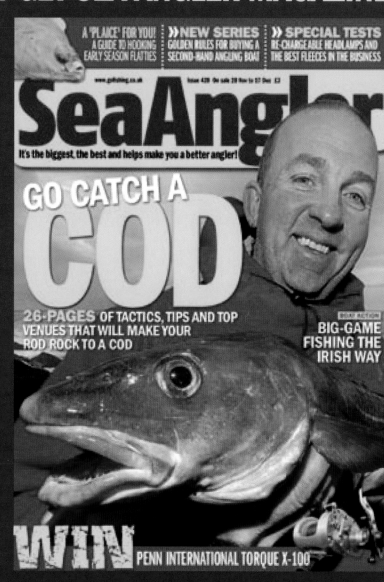

SHORE TERMINAL RIGS

A fundamental principle of the terminal rig is that it should follow a proven design which prevents it from tangling during fishing. It should include a link for attaching the lead and a clip or swivel to link it to the main line.

The most successful and popular design of rig for shore angling is the monofilament paternoster. This involves a main rig body line with hooklengths (snoods) coming off it at intervals via small swivels crimped in place between two micro beads.
This simple mono paternoster design is the basis of most of the popular shore angling terminal rigs we see today.

Making your own terminal rigs is a valuable skill for the sea angler because of the options it permits, such as different designs, dimensions and hook sizes. However, the relative dimensions of all rig elements are crucial to their performance, in that hooklengths should not be allowed to overlap each other or the top and bottom links. The beginner can copy a few shop-tied rigs to get the basic rules and construction ideas.

Fewer hooks on a rig means it has less chance of snagging on weed or rocks, but it also means your odds of catching fish are reduced. There is a fine balance in this initial decision, which is governed by the type of sea bed and the size of the species sought. Successfully fishing over a snaggy sea bed is often only possible with a single bait, either with one hook or two hooks (called a Pennell rig) in the same bait. The use of a large bait increases the scent trail and greatly improves the odds of a fish finding the bait in a forest of kelp, for example.

Over clear sand or mud, three hooks increase the odds of a fish taking the bait, and this tactic is particularly successful when fishing for small fish from piers and beaches. Bait scent is again important, but three small scented baits can have the same scent trail and properties of attraction as a single large bait.

Next into the equation comes casting distance – one baited hook can be cast further than two or three, and the difference is all too apparent when casting into a head wind or with a flapper rig.
This is where the hooklengths (snoods) hang down from the body of the rig, allowing the baits to spin and flap during the cast – reducing distance dramatically.

In order to improve the aerodynamic performance of baited terminal rigs, bait clips are added to pin hookbaits close behind the lead and to the rig's body. Casting distance is less important over rough ground, because the further you cast, the greater the odds of hooking up. Tackle strength is the first criterion for rough ground to enable the end gear to escape snags and allow the angler to haul fish through rock and weed.

Tackle loss is also more expensive if it involves complicated and intricate rigs with extra accessories such as bait clips and the like.

Distance can be a priority over clear ground to reach a distant fish-holding feature, and clipped rigs are generally used for increased casting distance over clear sea beds, or in order to cast past snags to a clear bottom. They also help to keep delicate baits on the hook during power casting.

SAFETY

The dangers of a rig or shock leader breaking and allowing a 6oz lead to fly off into a group of anglers or the public could be horrific, so safety is a high priority if you build your own rigs.
The main body line of the rig needs to be the same breaking strain as the casting shock leader and in general, for power casting, a minimum of 60lb is used. For overhead casting, lighter line down to 30lb can be used, but it is not usual to go below that breaking strain for any beach-casting situation. Shock leader and rig breaking strain is calculated by multiplying the weight of the lead or sinker by 10, for example, 6oz lead x
10 = 60lb; 7oz lead x 10 = 70lb leader and rig line.

There are risks in repeatedly using the same terminal rig. Inevitable damage means rigs have to be replaced regularly, so keep an eye on their condition.

"Rig dimensions and design affect bait presentation"

"Maximum distance and clipped-down hookbaits are not the only way to catch fish. A big scented bait will attract fish to it!"

THE BASIC RIG MAKING TOOLS

Simplicity is the secret of most terminal rigs, and the basic tools required to construct your own rigs are few and uncomplicated.

LINE CLIPPERS

The most essential tool of the rig maker, a pair of nail clippers, ensures that all knots are trimmed close. Hooks and swivels that sprout a long tag of monofilament are not only unsightly to the rig purist, but they put fish off the bait or collect weed on the rig. Fish bumping into the short spike of mono may not be deterred from eating the bait, but if they are, then that's a fish missed – better to trim knots close after they have been fully tightened. The clippers can also be used to cut the end of your mono at a sharp angle to assist with the threading of beads, crimps etc. They will also cut wire line, although this tends to wear them out quickly.

Available in several sizes, the largest clippers are the most efficient. They are, though, made mainly in the Far East in cheap chrome plate steel and tend to rust, blunt and get lost in the tackle box. Look out for a tough new set of stainless clippers from Fox!

RIG MEASURE

Special rig jigs are available, or you can use a tape measure to set the length of your rig and keep snoods uniform. However, a measure is not essential in rig construction. Experience allows you to judge lengths of snoods etc so that they do not overlap or tangle. The overall length of a rig, for instance, can be 6ft – the length of your outstretched arms. Snoods can vary between a few inches and several feet long. The rules on this are simple – there are no rules!

CRIMPING PLIERS AND PLIERS

Crimping pliers ensure that crimps are closed, but not crushed too tightly. If they were, they would damage the rig's main line, a point to beware of when using other types of pliers. Crimping pliers can also be used for pulling knots tight on hooks and swivels – especially hooks, which can slip if you hold them in your fingers. Never hold hooks in your teeth or mouth to tension knots, this is asking for an accident! Pliers are also ideal for opening the eye of a lead link or metal boom so that a swivel can be added; offsetting hook points; or bending the eye of a hook for use with a Pennell rig.

ODD TOOLS

Cigarette lighter: Used to blob/melt ends of knots, joints to braid line etc.

Braid scissors: These are essential if you are using braid, which is difficult to trim close with ordinary scissors or clippers.

Side cutters or pliers: Strong side cutters may be required for cutting stainless steel wire, etc.

Hook puller: A safer way of pulling knots tight. Avoid putting hooks near your mouth to tighten knots – it's Russian roulette, and sooner or later you will get a bite!

Leatherman-type multi-tool: Useful for odd angling jobs. The best ones are stainless steel which resist corrosion if left in the tackle box.

Felt tip pen: Used to permanently mark rig bags with the contents.

Others: Other essentials for shore angling include a sharp filleting knife and a pair of rust resistant scissors.

RIG WALLETS AND STORAGE

Detachable terminal rigs offer the shore angler a way of overcoming several problems encountered when fishing. First, if terminal tackle is damaged, tangled or lost it can be replaced in an instant – simply clip on a new rig. This saves lots of time when the fish are feeding, because a spare rig can be ready baited prior to each cast, while the option to change the rig type, number and size of hooks etc also brings advantages.

Two efficient ways to store terminal rigs include the popular rig wallet and the increasingly popular foam winder which comes from the Continent.

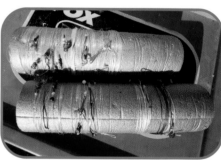

A section of foam pipe lagging is a handy DIY rig winder.

Rig wallets come in a range of sizes and designs, some with extra compartments for your terminal accessories, line and rig-making tools. You can expand the capacity of a rig wallet by storing each individual rig in a sealable plastic bag. This keeps the wallet clean when you return a used rig to it. Coiling the rig around your hand is a popular way to store it in a rig bag, although it is likely to tangle unless removed with care. Wrapping the rig around a piece of card can improve ease of removal. Marking your rig bags with the content, such as number of hooks, size, rig type etc improves efficiency. Some anglers use coloured beads of snood line to relate to rig type etc.

Growing in popularity are the Continental rig winders. These are particularly efficient for storing the longer, lighter line rigs used by match anglers, and are far less prone to tangling than conventional rig bags.

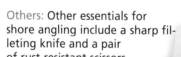

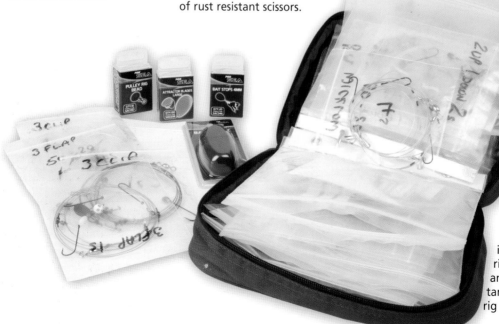

SOME BASIC RIG COMPONENTS

Terminal rig components and accessories are forever changing, with new ideas coming to the sea angling scene regularly. The rigs in this book include the latest ideas and options, but first here are a few terms and names to help you along.

Rig body line: Specialist co-polymer rig lines are becoming more readily available. These have less coiling 'memory' and often more knock strength, and are smoother for knot tying.

Snood line: Similarly, special snood lines are produced that combat the twists and damage caused by small fish and the marine environment.

Swivels: There are a range of types and sizes, with some having a mix of round and diamond eyes specifically for use tying rigs. A minimum of 60lb-plus is recommended for joining rigs to main line etc, while 45lb swivels are standard for hook snoods. Lighter, smaller swivels can be used on some terminal rigs when required. Swivel selection includes round and diamond eye, black and stainless from Fox, Berkley, Mustad and Gemini.

Clips and lead links: Gemini Genie lead links are required for sinkers and main line quick links.

Crimps: These come in a rage of styles from lots of manufacturers. Short, soft copper crimps or stainless steel are preferred because they do not corrode or damage the line. Plain steel crimps tend to rust.

Beads: Small micro beads are available from manufacturers like Fox and Gemini, and various tackle dealers. Larger beads can be used as snood stops, or to add attraction to bait. Float beads can be used to raise baits clear of crabs, or to add buoyancy to a bait.

Sequins and blades: 2cm-plus sequins and Fox blades in a range of colours can be used for bait stops, or as fish-attractors on hook snoods.

Power Gum: This stretchy material in 15lb to 20lb breaking strain, and in many colours, is used to form a stop knot on the rig. Drennan and Fox brands are preferred. Power gum stop knots have a number of uses on the rigs shown here. Mono line can also be used. Telephone wire is a stop gap for an emergency stop knot – available in lots of colours, it is simply twisted around the hook snood.

Rig tubing: Fox Silicone tubing has a host of uses, from making rigs, to bait stops, to snood stand-offs, in all colours.

Bait clip swivels: Fox and Breakaway (Cascade) swivels with built in bait clips are used for all clipped rigs. In multiples they release simultaneously.

Bait clips: The Breakaway Bait Shield and the Imp Clip are considered the two best bait clip devices after the Impact lead.

Breakaway Impact Lead: Considered the most efficient and fail safe of all bait clip devices – the release clip is moulded into the lead.

Snood clip: This is small clip device takes the place of a swivel on rigs. It is used to secure a hook snood via a short length of tubing.

ONE, TWO OR THREE HOOK FLAPPER

"A link and swivel can be used at the top of the rig to allow rigs to be changed or removed quickly from the main line."

"Rigs for shore casting usually employ a longer snood at the top of the rig to ensure that the hook bait is on the sea bed. This is especially important when fishing from piers or at short range. The majority of UK species like their food hard on the sea bed."

ONE, TWO OR THREE HOOK FLAPPER

The most basic terminal rig used by sea anglers is the mono flapper paternoster which can be used with one, two or three hooks.

The three hook version is ideal for fishing for the small species such as pouting, whiting, dab, flounder, codling, dogfish etc over clean or mixed ground from beaches or piers. Generally hook sizes between 2 and 1/0 are preferred, with strong patterns like the Fox or Kamasan Aberdeen offering a degree of safety should a large fish be hooked, while softer patterns that bend can be used to assist escape from a snag or for catch and release.

Rig dimensions: Rig body length 6ft, snood lengths inside 24 inches (all approximate and to suit different venues and species).

Build tips: Crimps are set lightly to allow the snood positions to be moved while fishing. Lower crimps can be replaced with a Power Gum stop knot. Rig clips can be used instead of swivels.

Best used for: General fishing for small species over clean to mixed sea beds. Often a compromise of just one or two hooks is used over mixed or snaggy ground.

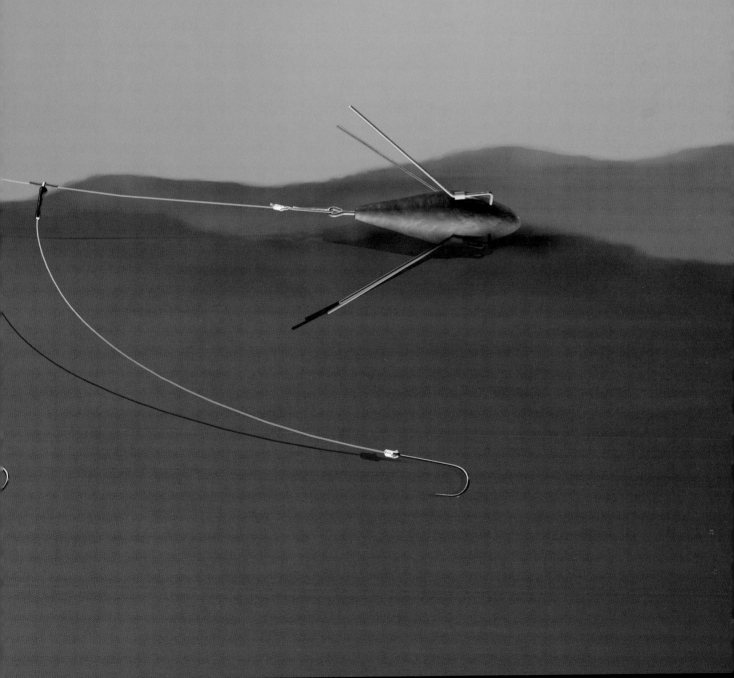

How to make a One, Two or Three Hook Flapper

Cut the rig body line at an angle with line clippers or a craft knife so it has a sharp point. This assists the threading of components such as beads and crimps. Thread on a crimp followed by a micro bead then one of the snood swivels (45lb), then another bead and another crimp.

Repeat this for each hook snood you want to create (the system is the same for one, two or three hook flapper rigs). Next tie a Genie lead link to the end of the line using a two or three turn Grinner knot. Some smooth co-polymer lines require three or even four turns.

Measure out the length of the rig (between 3ft and 6ft, this is optional and depends on how long you want the hook snoods. Your outstretched arms are a handy guide to rig length – an alternative is to measure off the length. Next, tie on the top clip/swivel, position the swivels equally along the length of the rig and secure in place by lightly crushing the crimps. Pinched lightly they will not damage the line and can be moved up and down the rig, allowing for adjustment of the hook snood positions. Some anglers prefer a Power Gum stop knot on the lower side of the swivel/bead to allow for more adjustment. One word about the gap you leave between crimp, bead and swivel.

Cut the line at a sharp angle to help with the threading of beads, crimps, swivels etc.

Thread on a crimp, a micro bead, a swivel, another micro bead and a crimp.

Crimps are fixed in position with crimping pliers. Be careful not to damage line.

Repeat for other snood swivel positions, spacing them equally over the length of the rig.

Tie on a lead link using a three turn Grinner knot.

Pull the knot tight slowly to prevent friction damaging line, then cut off tag end.

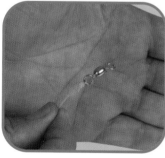

Repeat the same knot for the swivel at the top of the rig.

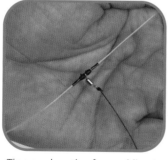

Tie on a length of snood line to each swivel. Using a three turn Grinner knot.

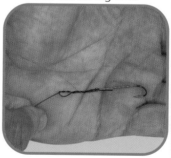

Tie a hook on the end of each snood, using a five turn half blood knot or three turn Grinner.

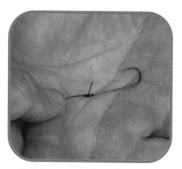

Pull knot together slowly and cut off tag end.

This rig configuration is perfect for fishing worm baits on size 1 hooks for the smaller species.

Some like the swivel to be gripped tightly so that it sticks out at right angles to the main line. Others prefer a gap, so that the swivel and beads can move between the crimps.
The choice is optional and has little effect on the rig's behaviour, although a large gap between the top snood crimps allows the snood to travel back up the rig line during the cast and this idea can be used to spread the hook-baits wider. Next, tie the hook snoods on the swivels using a three turn Grinner knot. Hook snood lengths are important in relation to the swivels' spacing on the rig's main line. Do not allow the hooks to overlap the swivel below, or the lead link, otherwise they will tangle.

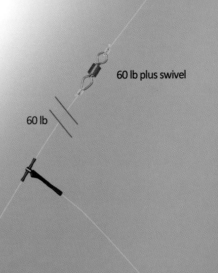

60 lb plus swivel

60 lb

Crimp

Crimp

Snood Clip

Silicone Sleeving

20 lb

Gemini Genie Lead Link

Breakout Lead

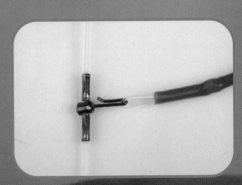

"Rigs can be constructed using rig swivels or snood clips, both secured with crimps or beads and crimps."

ONE, TWO OR THREE HOOK CLIPPED

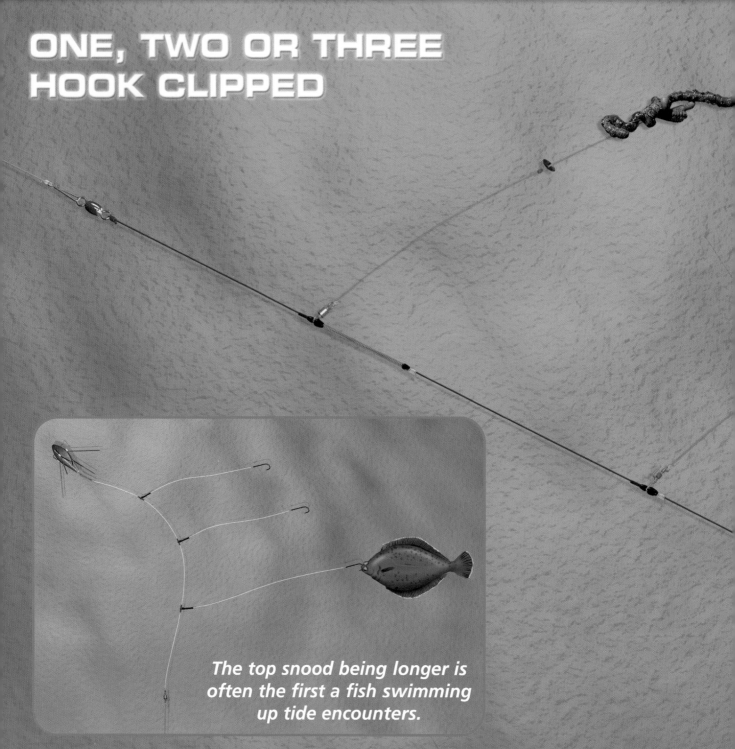

The top snood being longer is often the first a fish swimming up tide encounters.

ONE, TWO OR THREE HOOK CLIPPED

The same basic paternoster build as the three hook flapper, but using Breakaway Cascade swivels or similar for the hook snoods and a Breakaway Impact lead, or Imp bait clip on the lead link.
Can be used with one, two or three hooks for fishing at long range.

Rig dimensions: Body length 6ft, hook snoods under 24 inches (subject to venue, species, conditions etc).

Build tips: Instead of using crimps, stop knots tied in Power Gum or monofilament can be used to hold the hook snood swivels in position. These allow adjustment of the snoods to fit the bait clips – very useful if hook snoods are changed or replaced. Clipped rigs require the addition of a bait stop on each hook snood to prevent the bait travelling up the hook snood away from the hook. Adding an tension spring below the top snood swivel tensions the hooks in the clips and helps prevent them releasing prematurely.

Best used for: Long range casting and on occasions for casting with delicate worm baits.

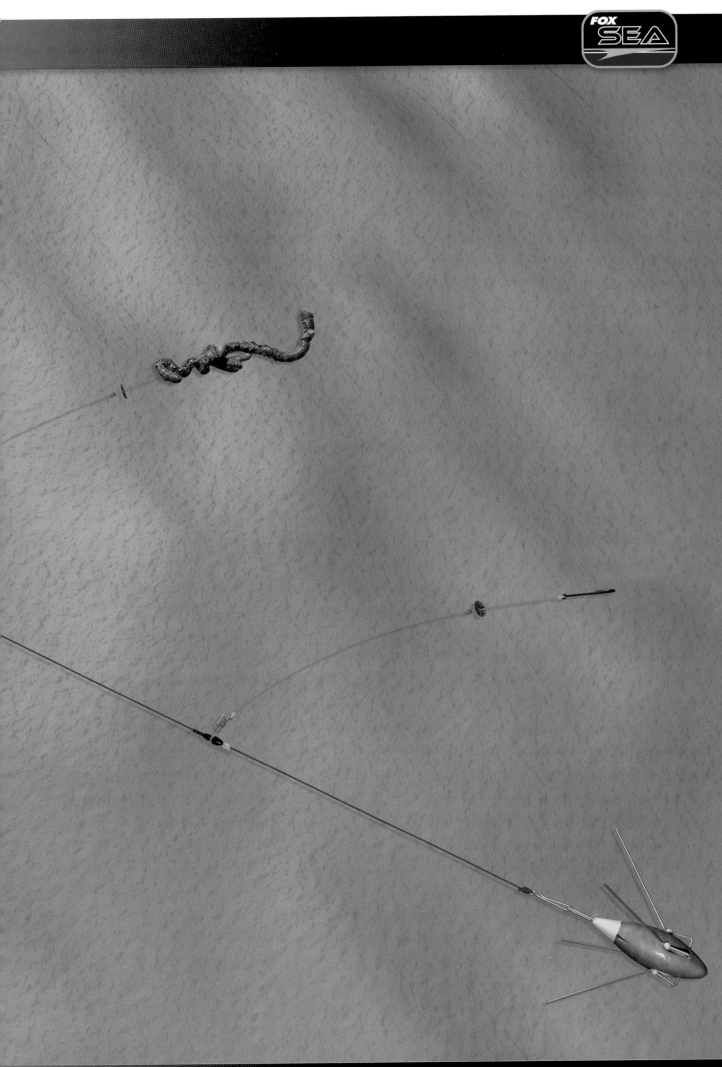

How to make a One, Two or Three Hook Clipped

Cut the rig body line at an angle with a line clipper so it has a sharp point. This improves the ease of threading of components such as beads and crimps.

Thread on a crimp followed by a bead then the snood swivel, then another bead, then a tension spring and another bead. A Power Gum stop knot (three turn Grinner) is tied here later.

Next thread on another crimp, a micro bead, a cascade swivel and then a bead. A Power Gum stop knot is tied here later. Repeat for a three hook rig (the system is the same for, one or two hook flapper rigs). Next, tie the Genie lead link to the end of the rig main line.
Measure out the length of the rig (between 3ft and 6ft is usual) and depends upon how long you want the hook snoods. Tie on the top clip or swivel using a Grinner knot.

Next position the swivels equally along the length of the rig and secure in place by lightly crushing the crimps which are above each of the snood swivels. Pinched lightly, they will not damage the line and can be moved up and down the rig to allow adjustment of the hook snood positions. The hook snoods are tied to each swivel later.

Next tie on the Power Gum stop knots (four turn Grinner) on the lower side of each bead below a swivel as previously mentioned. These hold the swivel in position and can be used later to position the hook snood precisely.
Crimps can be also used here, but they can damage the line when moved up and down the rig line and jam if closed too tightly, preventing adjustment of the hook fitting the bait clip.

The tension spring fitted under the top hook swivel is crucial because it tensions the clipped hook snoods over the length of the rig and prevents them unclipping during the cast. You only need one SRT spring under the top hook snood swivel!

Next tie the hook snoods on the three swivels down the rig using a three turn Grinner knot. Hook snood lengths are important in relation to the clip below, so tie on hooks approximately to that length. Before you tie on the hooks add a Fox bait stop and sequin or bead – alternatively a 1cm length of silicone tubing – followed by a sequin to each. This forms a bait stop which prevents the bait running up the snood away from the hook during the cast. Pass the snood line through the silicone tube twice to form a loop, pull tight and the stop will be formed. Next, thread on a sequin and then tie on the hook.
Hang the rig up and clip on the Impact lead, and adjust snood/hook positions by sliding Power Gum stops up or down (wetting them makes them slide more easily), then tighten top crimps.

Cut the line at a sharp angle to aid the threading of beads, crimps, swivels etc.

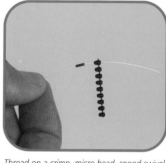
Thread on a crimp, micro bead, snood swivel, micro bead, tension Spring and bead. This will be secured later with a stop knot.

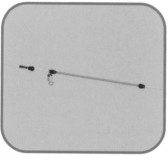
The tension spring is included on the top swivel only.

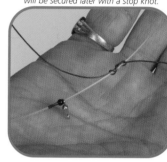
Use a three to four turn Grinner knot to secure hook swivels in position.

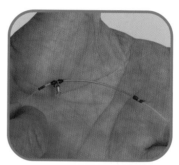
The stop knot allows adjustment of position and tension of the tension spring.

The remaining two swivels are Cascade type with built-in bait clip. Secure lower side with stop knot.

Add snood to all rig swivels.

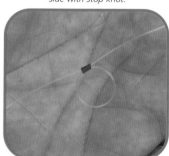
A bait stop is included on all hook snoods. Take a small section of silicone tube and thread line through twice.

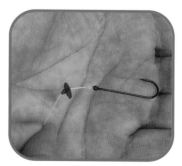
Pull stop tight and add sequin, then tie hook with half blood knot.

Hooks clip into the clip below. The lower hook clips into the impact lead.

"Beware – hook snood and rig body length should be in proportion. Change one element and it will affect the other"

60lb + Swivel

Crimp

Plain 40lb swivel

Tension Spring

Power Gum or mono stop knot

20lb +

Bait stop

Sequin

Cascade swivel

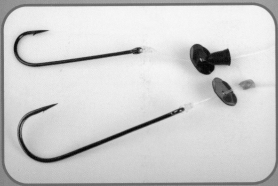

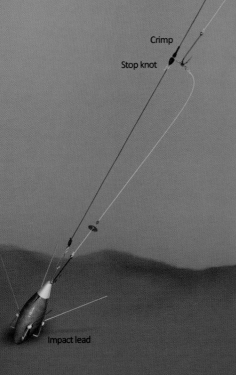

"A Fox bait stop and sequin (top) and a silicone tubing bait stop and sequin (bottom)."

Crimp

Stop knot

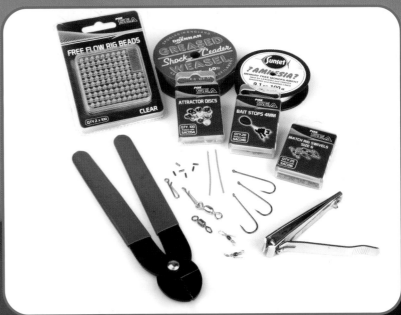

Impact lead

51

PULLEY RIG

PULLEY RIG

Primarily for fishing over rough ground and for larger fish like cod, bass, smoothhound and ray.
The principle of this rig is that it is simple, streamlined and offers better odds of retrieve with a fish on.
The weight of the fish on what is effectively a running paternoster lifts the lead as it is retrieved, lessening the
likelihood of it catching snags. There are variations of design of this rig and it can be used with a single
hook (2/0 to 6/0) or two hooks in a Pennell rig configuration which uses two hooks (2/0 to 6/0) in a single large bait.
It is also used with a Wishbone design. Terminal rigs designed for use over snaggy venues are not
fail-safe, and it is the angler's tackle and technique, especially retrieval, which are often far more important than the rig
design. A strong main line, a well loaded reel and a fast retrieve are essential.

Body length: Usually between 3ft and 5ft, dependant on the length of the hook snood required.
The shorter snood length will stay on the bait clip better in windy conditions

Build tips: Make sure that the hook snood length is strong enough if power casting. Check out the new Fox Pulley rig beads which
are ideal for this rig.

Best used for: A big-fish rig, as well as a 'get out of jail' rig for the most extreme rough ground venues. The one rig that will not
come unclipped before it hits the sea in the most extreme weather!

"Using a conventional paternoster rig over rough ground, when a fish is being retrieved the lead bumps along the sea bed and can snag. Using a pulley rig the weight of the fish pulls the lead to the top of the rig away from the sea bed."

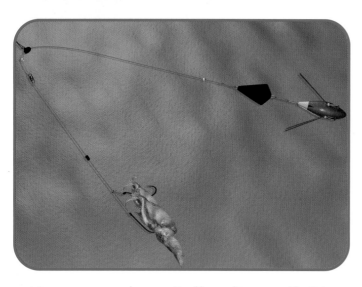

How to make a Pulley (Pennell) Rig

Tie on a Genie lead link to the end of the rig main line using a two or three turn Grinner knot. Measure the length of the rig required. Remember, a longer hook snood requires a pro-portionally longer rig body length. Normal maximum length is four feet. Next thread on a rig bead, a Fox Pulley bead and another rig bead. Tie on a 60lb-plus swivel.

The hook snood is tied to the end of the 60lb-plus rig swivel with a three turn Grinner knot. Hook snood breaking strain should be strong enough to take the strain of casting, because with this rig casting pressure is put on the hook snood – 40lb is usually the absolute minimum breaking strain for a Pulley rig hook snood. You will need to add a bait stop to the snood before tying on the hook or hooks. The Pulley rig includes the use of an Impact lead with bait clip or another bait clip device such as the Breakaway Imp.

*The Pennell rig involves two hooks on a single snood. One slides on the snood line above the other, which is tied to the end of the snood. Offsetting the eye of the sliding hook helps it slide along the snood more efficiently. The sliding hook can be secured on the snood by wrapping the snood line around it or by adding a small length of silicone tubing.

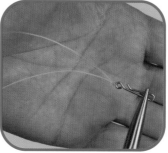

Tie a Genie lead link to the end of the rig line using a three turn Grinner knot.

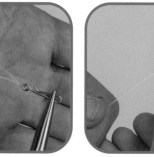

Measure the length of rig required and cut line at angle to aid threading of beads etc.

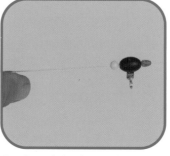

Thread on a rig bead, Fox Pulley bead and then another rig bead to act as a buffer. You can use Fox Bait Stops instead.

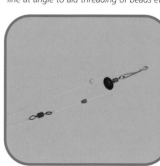

Tie a rig swivel to the other end of the line.

Tie the hook snood on to the swivel and then tie on the hook.

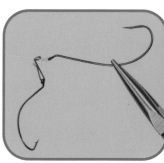

For a Pennell rig, slide another hook on to the snood before tying the first hook on the end.

The Fox Pennell Clip is the most efficient Pennell rig fixing. Alternatives are rubber tub-ing or simply wrapping line around the hook shank.

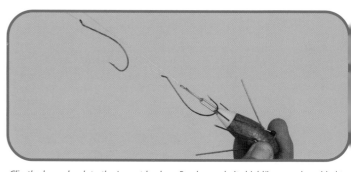

Clip the lower hook to the Impact lead – a Breakaway bait shield/imp can be added to clip down the rig with any other type of lead.

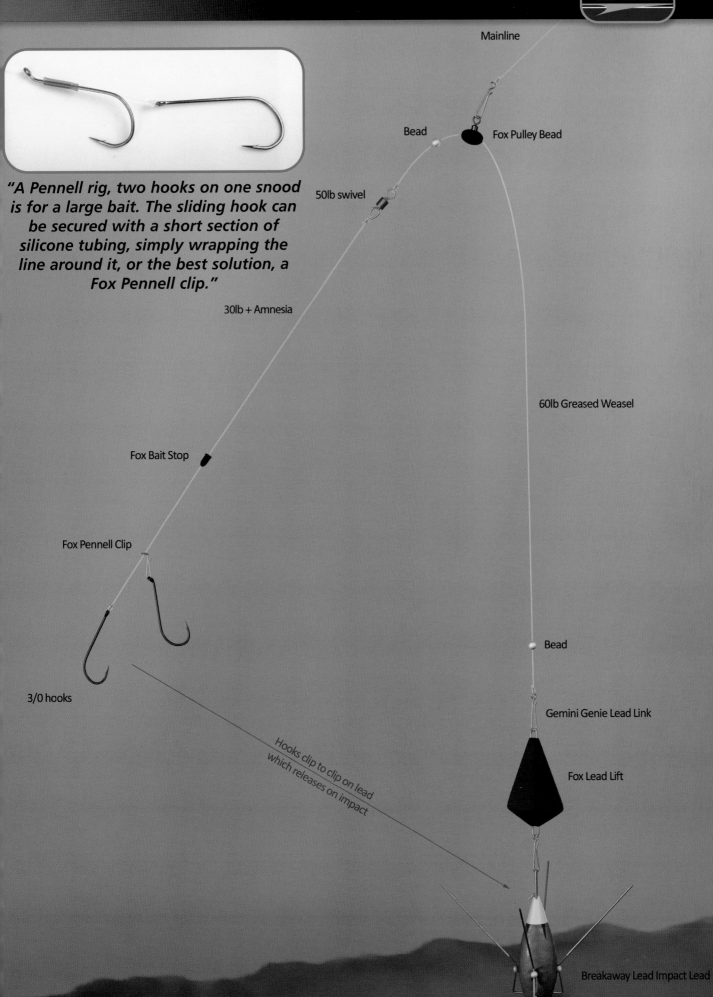

"A Pennell rig, two hooks on one snood is for a large bait. The sliding hook can be secured with a short section of silicone tubing, simply wrapping the line around it, or the best solution, a Fox Pennell clip."

Mainline

Bead

Fox Pulley Bead

50lb swivel

30lb + Amnesia

60lb Greased Weasel

Fox Bait Stop

Fox Pennell Clip

Bead

3/0 hooks

Gemini Genie Lead Link

Hooks clip to clip on lead which releases on impact

Fox Lead Lift

Breakaway Lead Impact Lead

THREE WIRE BOOM RIG

THREE WIRE BOOM RIG

Boom rigs are popular for short and medium range work only, although Gemini produces a clipped down boom for power casting. The three standard wire or plastic booms chosen by many anglers add weight to the rig and restrict distance, but they nail baits to the sea bed and the wire booms are said to give off a faint electrical current which fish can pick up. The ideal rig for using very light hook snoods between 5lb and 20lb, the booms prevent tangles with the rig body (subject to them being correct length).

Body lengths: Generally 6ft, longer for surf when casting with long rods. Snood length is kept to 12in or under.

Build tips: Add a small 30lb swivel to the end of booms to help prevent small fish spinning off hook snoods. This can be secured with a length of tubing. This rig can be constructed as three booms up or with a boom close to the lead so one snood can be fished below the lead (known as down).

Best used for: Highly favoured for flounder fishing, or for match fishing when the going is tough (scratching), and in conjunction with a feeder.

Longer, French-style wire booms can also be used to present baits alongside a pier wall for pollack, scad, bass and wrasse.

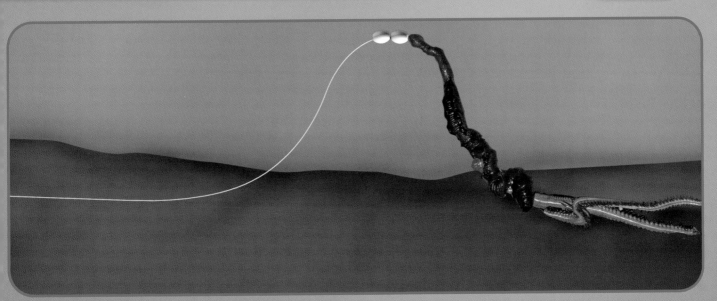

"Floating/Buoyant beads can be used to raise a bait off the sea bed. This allows them to be influenced by any water movement caused by a fish etc, thus adding attraction to the bait. Add extra floating beads to the hook snood to raise the bait completely off the sea bed away from hungry crabs"

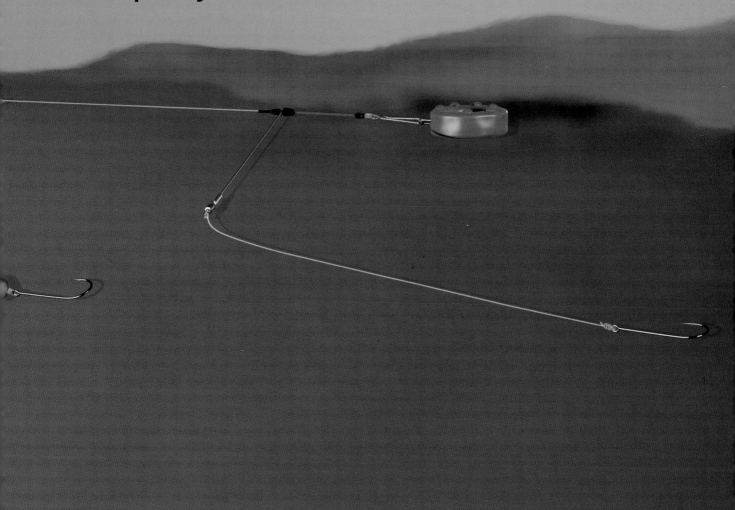

How to make a Three Wire Boom Rig

Fit small swivels to the end of each of the wire booms, cut a short length of 2mm rig tubing (2cm/3cm long) and slide it over the eye of the boom. Then open up the eye of the boom with pliers and insert the swivel. Close the eye carefully and then slide the rig tubing back along the boom on to the eye and body of the swivel. The rig tubing supports the swivel and helps position the hook snood straight out from the end of the boom.

Next, cut the main rig line at an angle with line clippers – this aids the threading of beads, crimps etc. Slide on a crimp, then a bead, the boom, another bead, the tension spring, another bead and finally a crimp. Repeat this for all three booms. It's essential that an tension spring is positioned below each boom. Slightly compressed, this holds the boom up, at right angles to the rig body line.

Once all the booms are on the rig body line, tie on a Genie lead link to the end of the line using a three turn Grinner knot and measure the rig line to the length required. A standard measurement is the outstretched arms (6ft), although a rig length of 4ft is sufficient for pier fishing etc. Next tie the top swivel to the top of the rig using a two or three turn Grinner knot. Positioning of the booms is then a matter of spacing them equally over the length of the rig. Close crimps gently so that the tension springs are slightly compressed and support the booms.

You can also use stop knots made from Power Gum on the lower side of each boom to allow for adjustment, as in several of the other rigs in the series.

Next tie the hook snoods to the small swivels, and add the hooks. The length of the snoods should be just short of the boom below, or, in the case of the lowest snood, the lead. Snoods using Genie booms can be longer overall (including boom) than those on a monofilament paternoster because the boom stands out from the rig, lifting it away from the lower boom. However, remember that large or heavy hookbaits will cause the boom to droop and tangle and so lengths should be adjusted to suit the baits being used. Plastic booms can also be used if preferred, and Gemini rig booms are available in a clipped down version.

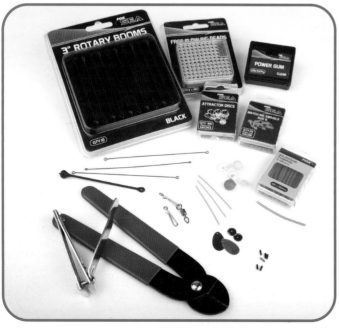

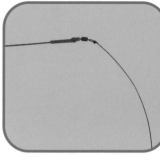

Add a small swivel to the eye of each boom.

Secure with a short length of Silicone tubing. Add hook snood.

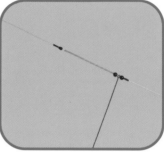

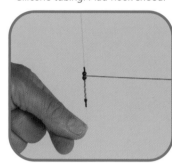

Thread each boom on the rig line. Complete with crimps, beads and tension spring.

Crimped boom in position on main line so that the tension spring is compressed.

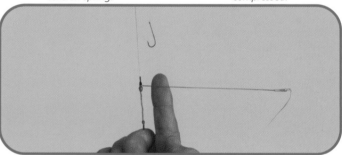

Tie on hooks, making sure they do not overlap the boom below.

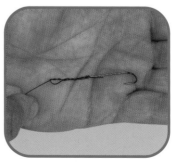

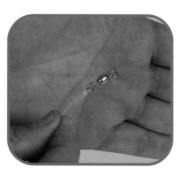

Add swivel to the top of rig.

Add lead link to the bottom of rig.

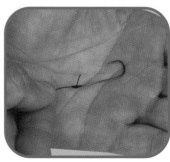

Tie on hooks with a half blood knot.

Cut off tag end. Booms allow the use of low-diameter hook snoods.

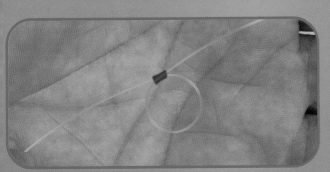

"Bait stops are available from Fox. The DIY version (above) is constructed using a 1cm length of silicone tubing."

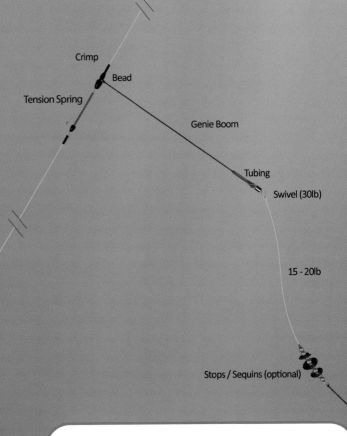

50lb+

Crimp

Bead

Tension Spring

Genie Boom

Tubing

Swivel (30lb)

15 - 20lb

Glow Bead (optional)

Stops / Sequins (optional)

Genie Leadlink

Plain Bomb, Grip or
Watch Lead (shown)
optional choice

"Beads and sequins add both a visual and sound attractor to hook baits, great for flatties."

"Wire or plastic booms allow very light hook snoods to be used, beware of making them too long."

TWO UP ONE DOWN FLAPPER RIG

"A two up, one down terminal rig, either flapper or clipped, is the world's most efficient rig. Compact and balanced it allows baits to be presented both on and near the bottom."

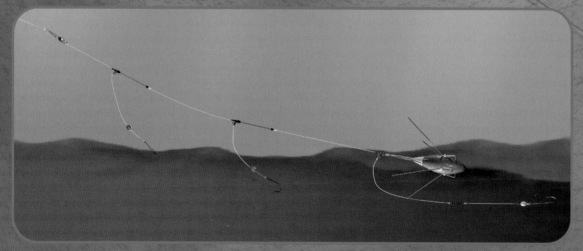

TWO UP ONE DOWN FLAPPER RIG

This is a variation of the three hook flapper, with the lower snood coming off the rig just above the lead link. Ideal for fishing for flatfish, it is considered to be one of the best all-round rigs, because its make-up spreads the hookbaits over the widest possible area. It is popular for flounder fishing at close range, and an ideal design for use when long hook snoods are preferred. Hook sizes between 2 and 1/0 are best, with strong patterns like the Fox or Kamasan Aberdeen offering a degree of safety should a large fish be hooked.

Rig dimensions: Rig body length 6ft-plus, snood lengths 30 inches-plus (all approximate and to suit different venues and species).

Build tips: Crimps set lightly allow the snood positions to be moved. Alternatively, on this rig variation, use Power Gum or mono stop knots to secure snood swivels in position. These can then be moved so that a three hook flapper rig can be converted into a two up, one down rig in an instant simply by moving the lower snood down to the lead link. Rig clips can be used instead of swivels.

Best used for: General fishing for small species over clean to mixed sea beds. Great for a long surf when hooks need spacing as wide as possible and for fishing alongside pier walls and structures for pollack, scad and mullet.

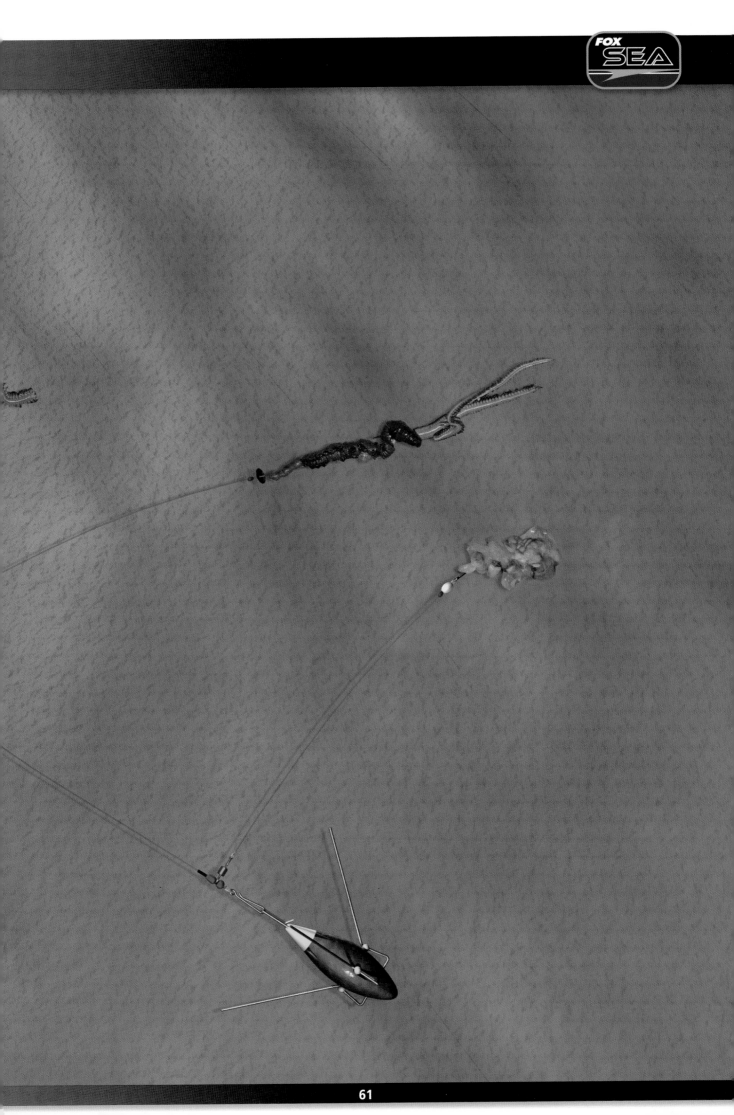

How to make a Two Up One Down Flapper Rig

Cut the rig body line at an angle with line clippers so it has a sharp point. This assists the threading on of components such as beads and crimps. Thread on a crimp followed by a micro bead then one of the 30lb swivels, another micro bead and another crimp. Repeat for the second hook snood position. Now add another crimp and then another micro bead, a swivel, yet another micro bead and a final crimp. (A crimp below the lowest bead is not needed for this rig because the lower bead will settle against the knot that joins the lead link. However, if you want to change the rig during use to a three hook paternoster this crimp must be included). Next, tie the Genie lead link to the end of the rig line. The lower hook snood comes off the swivel directly above the lead link. Using a different coloured bead here on this type of rig will identify the rig as having a hook snood below the lead. Measure out the length of the rig (between 5ft and 6ft). Your outstretched arms are a handy guide to rig length, but an alternative is to measure off the length. Tie on the top clip/swivel.
Next, position the lower swivel close to the Genie lead link and close the crimp/s lightly. The second swivel should be crimped lightly top and bottom up the rig body and far enough above the lead link to allow the length of snood you want to

use (2ft is usual).
The third swivel is crimped lightly in position a similar distance from the second. Next, tie the hook snoods on the three swivels using a three turn Grinner knot. Hook snood lengths are important in relation to their spacing on the rig's body line. Do not allow the hooks to overlap the swivel below, or the lead link, otherwise they will tangle.

Because the crimps are not closed tightly, a degree of adjustment is possible for the hook snoods, allowing you to get the lengths and positions spot-on so that they hang without tangling.

Fox snood clips are an alternative to rig swivels. Secure the snoods via a loop and short length of rig tubing.

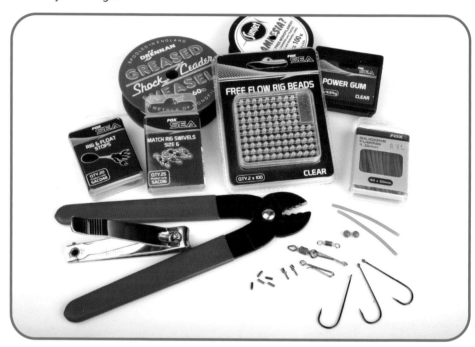

Cut the line at a sharp angle to help with the threading of beads, crimps, swivels etc.

Thread on a crimp, mirco bead, rig swivel, bead and crimp. (repeat for middle hook snood).

Close crimps lightly with the proper pliers for the job.

Lightly closed crimps allow snood position to be moved. You can also use a Power Gum stop knot.

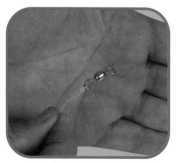

Tie on a swivel to top of rig.

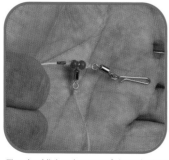

Tie a lead link to bottom of rig and crimp lower snood swivel close to it. Different coloured beads can be used to denote that the rig has a hook below the lead.

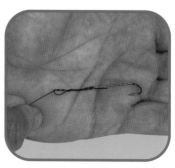

Add snoods to all three swivels and tie on hooks.

Cut tag end off close to hook eye. Otherwise, during casting, the bait will travel beyond the knot and become trapped on line away from the hook point.

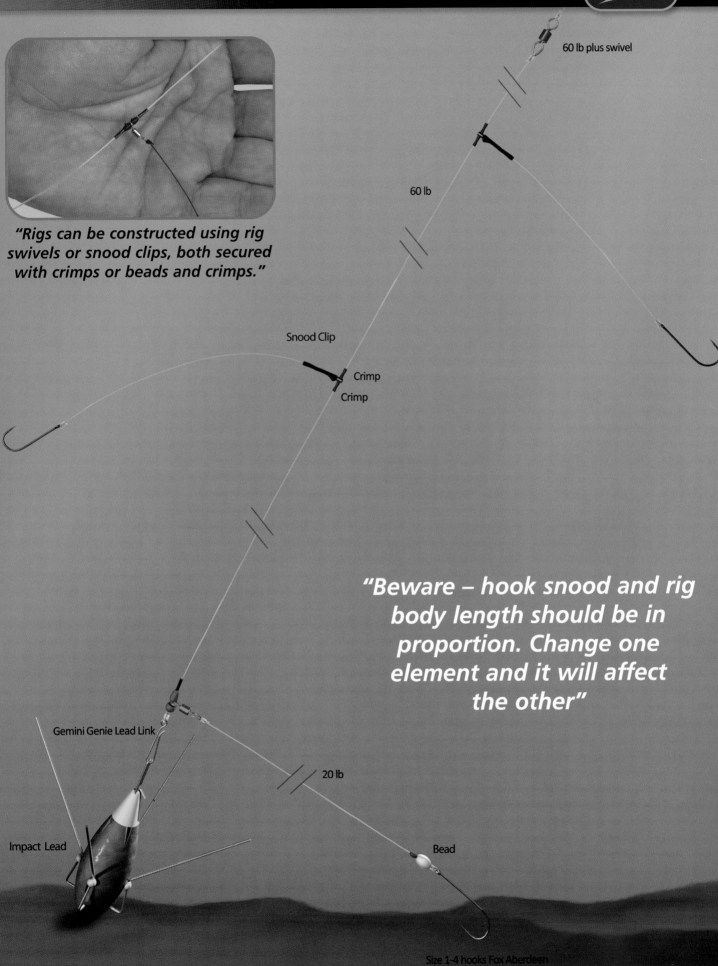

"Rigs can be constructed using rig swivels or snood clips, both secured with crimps or beads and crimps."

60 lb plus swivel

60 lb

Snood Clip

Crimp

Crimp

"Beware – hook snood and rig body length should be in proportion. Change one element and it will affect the other"

Gemini Genie Lead Link

20 lb

Impact Lead

Bead

Size 1-4 hooks Fox Aberdeen

TWO UP ONE DOWN CLIPPED LOOP RIG

TWO UP ONE DOWN CLIPPED LOOP RIG

This rig is the ultimate extreme range casting rig and can be used in two or three hook configurations from clear beaches and piers for all manner of species. For the smaller species like dogfish, dab, whiting, plaice, sole, pout etc, size 1 hooks are ideal. For codling, ray and smoothhound increase hook size to 3/0 or above.

Body length: 6ft for three hooks, 4ft for two.

Build tips: The rig is a two up, one down design with two hooks clipped directly behind the lead via an inline Cascade swivel in the lower snood. By placing an tension tension spring below both the upper swivels on a three hook rig it can be changed to a two hook rig by removing the top snood shore keep the advantage of the tension spring in tensioning snoods. Buying ready made rigs from the tackle shop to copy is a great way to discover how to construct the more complicated rigs like the Loop rig.

Best used for: Perfect for extreme range situations. No other rig allows three hooks to be cast so far. Many anglers consider this rig the equivalent to a two hook rig in terms of casting distance.

X **Middle snood too long**

TIDE DIRECTION

"Snood dimensions of the two up, one down terminal rig need to be adjusted so that they do not tangle or overlap in tide. The middle snood needs to be less than 50% or the length of the lower snood."

How to make a Two Up One Down Loop Rig

Cut the rig body line at an angle with line clippers so it has a sharp point. This assists with the threading of components such as beads and crimps. Thread on a crimp, followed by a bead, then one of the hook swivels, then another bead. Then thread on the tension spring and another bead. This is the top snood and will be secured with a Power Gum stop knot later in the sequence.

Now thread on another crimp followed by a bead and then a Cascade swivel and another bead. Next, thread a crimp, bead, swivel and second bead on the main line for the lower hook length, and tie the Genie lead link to the end of the line with a two/three turn Grinner knot.

Measure out the length of the rig (between 4ft and 6ft – exact length depends on how long you want the hook snoods to be. You can now tie a Power Gum stop knot, using a four turn Grinner knot, below the bead that holds the tension spring and the Cascade swivel. In extreme weather conditions two Power Gum stop knots can help prevent bait clips moving).

Cut the line at a sharp angle to aid the threading of beads, crimps, swivels etc.

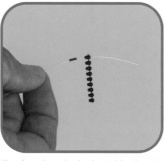

Thread on crimp, micro bead, swivel, bead, tension spring and another bead for the top snood. The remaining snood swivels are threaded on each complete with a crimp and beads. The midde swivel is a cascade swivel, with a built in bait clip.

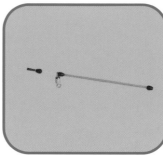

The tension spring on the top snood provides the tension to keep the hooks on the bait clip when casting.

Next, close the crimp at the bottom of the rig so that it secures the lower swivel between the beads as close as possible to the lead link.

Tie on around a 2ft length (exact length depens on how long you want lower snood) of 25lb mono to the lower swivel and to that tie on the Cascade swivel via the curved loop that would normally go on the rig main line. (For neatness you can straighten and shape the wire loop with pliers if you wish). Tie on a short (6ins) length of line to the Cascade swivel eye.

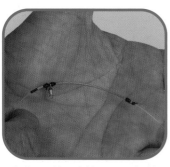

Fix the position of the top snood with tension spring with a stop knot (3 turn grinner) in mono or power gum.

The second hook snood comes off the rig via a cascade swivel secured by a crimp at the top and two mono or power gum stop knots underneath.

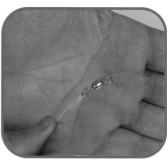

Tie on a 60lb + swivel to top of rig.

The top hook snood is tied on to the top swivel (2ft) Next, add the 1cm length of silicone tubing to each hook snood. Pass the line through the silicone tubing twice and it will lock on the line to form the bait stop. Add a sequin and then tie on the hook(s).

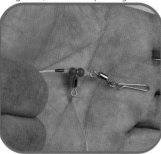

The lower hook snood comes off the swivel crimped close to the lead link.

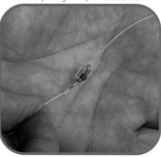

Tie a snood to the lower swivel and then a cascade swivel to its end. To that tie a short hook length and the hook.

The rig snood positions will need to be tensioned and adjusted to allow the rig to be clipped up properly. That is why Power Gum stop knots are used – these can be easily moved. (You can also use a crimp for securing the bottom side of the swivel, but these are far less adjustable than Power Gum stop knots and can damage the line if crushed too tightly).

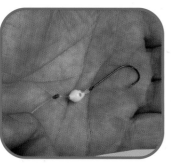

Tie hook snood's to the remaining swivels and add a Fox bait stop to each. This can be in the form of a sequin or a bead.

The power gum stop knots on the rig allow the snood positions to be altered up or down. This also allows hook snoods to be clipped tightly.

With the hooks clipped in position they are streamlined behind the lead. Adjustment to tension can be made via the top snood, stop knots and tension spring. The loop formed when the rig is clipped together has little or no effect on casting distance.

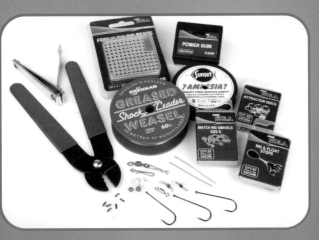

Gemini Genie Lead Link

60 lb+ Swivel

Crimp

Tension Spring

Stop knot

"Rig snood positions will need to be tensioned and adjusted to allow the rig to be clipped up properly. That is why Power Gum stop knots are used"

Bait Stop

Sequin

Cascade Swivel

This snood hangs loose in a loop hence rig name

60lb

20lb+

30lb swivel

Impact Lead

This hook clips to bait clip on impact lead

Aberdeen Hook

Cascade Swivel

"A cascade swivel placed in line on the lower snood is used to position the lower hook baits close behind an impact lead."

Bead

Fox Float Bead

SLIDING FLOAT RIG

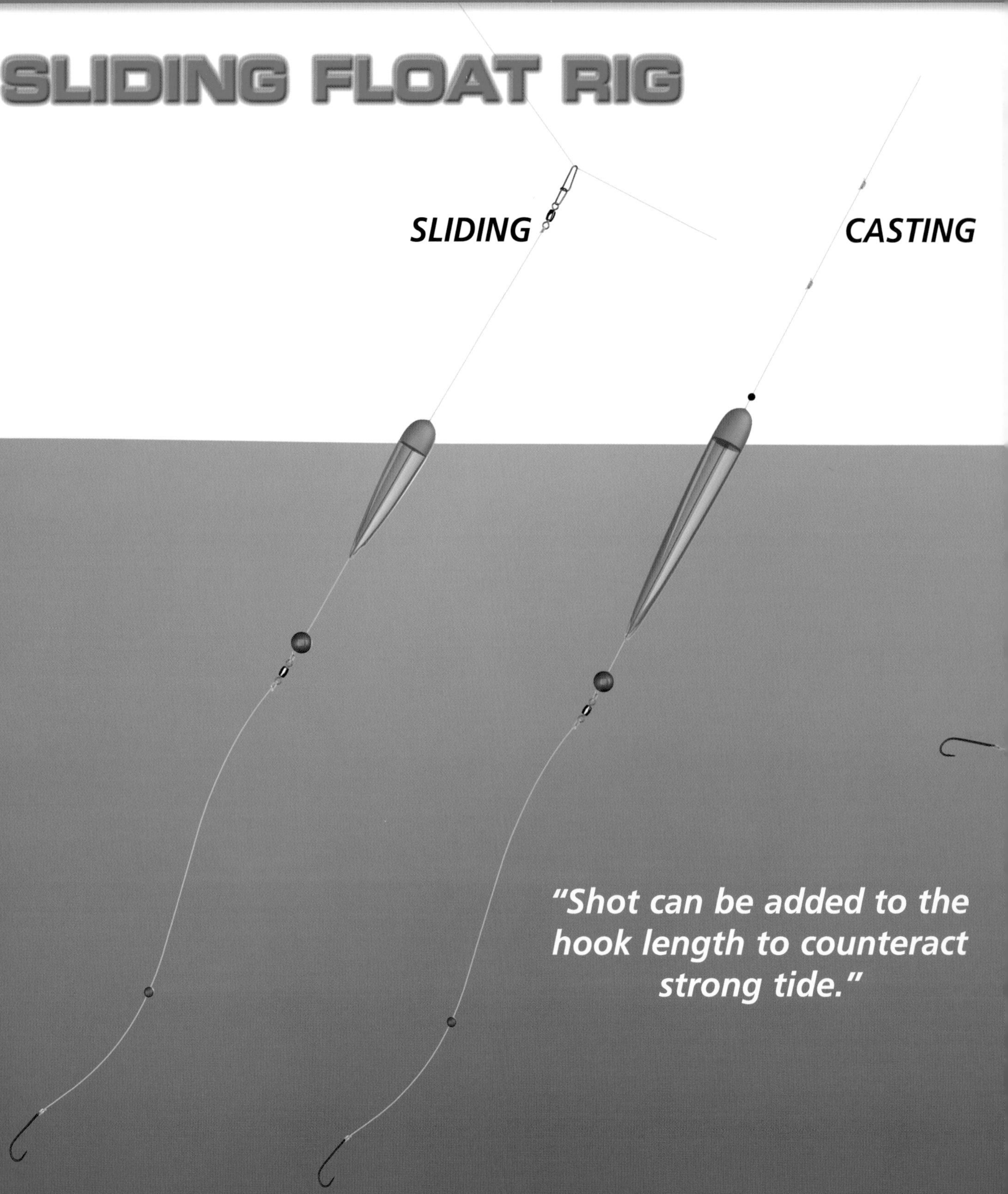

SLIDING

CASTING

"Shot can be added to the hook length to counteract strong tide."

"The depth the bait is fished can be crucial and is usually within 12ft of the surface."

SLIDING FLOAT RIG

This is the basic sliding float rig, used either direct to the main line on a lighter rod or as a terminal rig that can be slid down the main line of a rod already cast to catch mackerel, garfish etc. The latter effectively allows the angler to fish on the surface and the bottom at the same time.

Body length: This needs to be adjusted to suit the depth that the bait is required to be fished. On the casting float rig the depth can be set by a stop knot placed on the main line. This is moved to suit the tide and feeding depth of the species sought. On the sliding rig there is less scope for adjustment of depth, and the rig needs to be as long as the depth the bait is required to be fished.

Build tips: Use a bullet lead to cock the float, and add a stop knot above it to prevent it moving during the cast. A moving lead can cause the rig to tumble and tangle.

Best used for: Mainly for catching mid-water species off the sea bed – mackerel, garfish, scad, pollack, wrasse, bream, mullet, bass etc. For mullet, which are tackle-shy, a lighter line and smaller waggler float will be required.

How to make a Sliding Float Rig

The basic sliding float rig is simple enough to construct, with a cigar-shaped float with a hole throughout its length threaded on to the mainline above a bullet lead, and the line tied to the top of a swivel. The hooklength, approximately 3ft long, is tied to the bottom eye of the swivel and a moveable stop knot (two knots is a good idea when the depth is going to be continually adjusted) is fixed to the mainline above the float. This can then be then be pushed up or down the main line to adjust the depth the bait is fished below the float.

Adding a small bead above the float prevents the stop knot entering the hole through the float and jamming. The stop knot can be tied with a short length of monofilament line (use a line of lower diameter than the main line) or Power Gum, using a three or four turn Grinner knot. A cruder, but effective, method of making a tough stop knot is to use six turns of light telephone wire. Both travel easily through the rod rings back to the reel, allowing the rig to be cast.

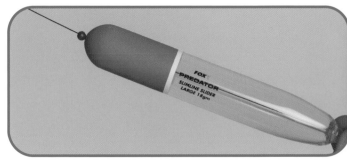

Thread the mainline through a bead and then through the float.

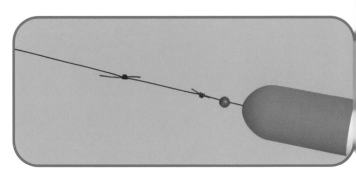

Add two stop knots above the bead (Power Gum or mono). This prevents the stops jamming in the float.

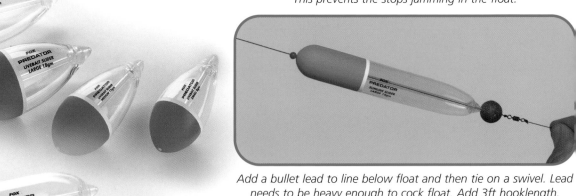

Add a bullet lead to line below float and then tie on a swivel. Lead needs to be heavy enough to cock float. Add 3ft hooklength.

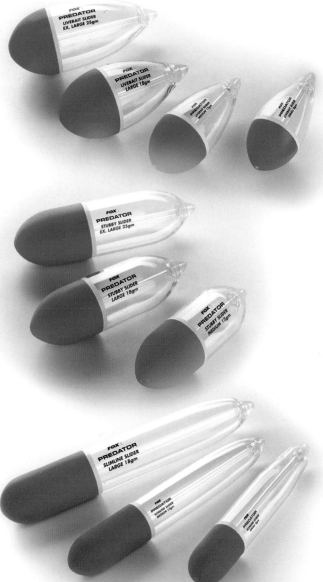

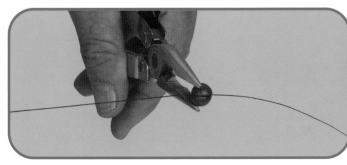

A split shot can be added to the hooklength to adjust how the float sits in the water or to keep bait down in the tide.

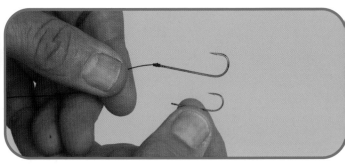

Add a hook – small sizes are used for garfish, more substantial ones for pollack, bass etc.

To rod

Slide down mainline

Mainline

American Snaplink

40lb

To rod

Mainline

Two mono or power gum stop knots

12 - 15lb

Float

Float

Drilled Bullet

Swivel 40lb

Drilled Bullet

Swivel 40lb

20lb

20lb

AAA Shot (optional for tide)

AAA Shot (optional for tide)

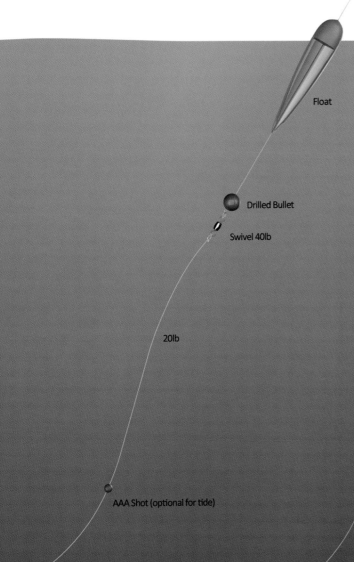

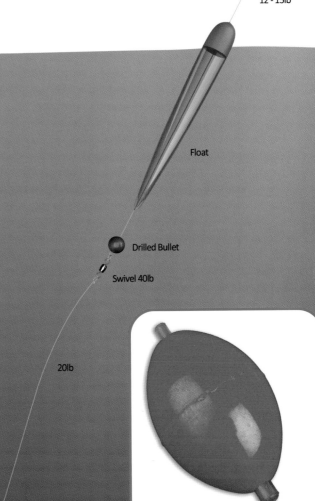

"A bubble float can be part filled with water to add weight for long casting with bait or lures."

STAGGERED WISHBONE RIG

"The wishbone rig can be constructed with hooks on seperate snoods or with both hooks on one main snood via a swivel. (see page 74)"

STAGGERED WISHBONE RIG

The original running wishbone rig was once popular for long-range fishing with a variety of baits, and first came into prominence as a plaice rig on the south coast. This updated version staggers the two hooks by using a cascade swivel behind the lead (as the loop rig) and is far more streamlined than the original wishbone design, which places the two hookbaits on the same clip. That way they tend to wobble or release early during the cast.

Body length: Up to 5ft with snood length between 18in and 36in.

Build tips: Stop knots and a Tension spring enable easy adjustment of the snood lengths and positions. Best suited to use with an Impact lead or Breakaway Imp bait clip. You can also add a Pennell (two hooks) to one of the two snoods.

Best used for: Ideal for casting long distances with mixed baits. A great rig for fishing for dogfish, codling and plaice, or match fishing at long range.

"The wishbone rig is prone to tangle and is best constructed with short hook snoods and only used in strong tide. It tangles more often during the retrieve without a fish on."

How to make a Staggered Wishbone Rig

The basis of the wishbone rig is a single 4ft or 5ft mono paternoster. Cut the rig body line at an angle and thread on a crimp, then a micro bead, a swivel and another bead. Add a tension spring below the lower bead on the rig body line and fix its position with a Power Gum stop knot (you can also use a lightly closed crimp). Tie a short length of snood line to the swivel. Next, tie a swivel/top clip to the top of the rig to enable it to be clipped easily to the reel main line. Tie a Genie lead link to the bottom of the rig to take the Breakaway Impact lead or Breakaway Imp. Rig length is optional, but as a guide it needs to be approximately twice as long as the snood. This prevents the hooks tangling with the top clip as the rig sinks after the hooks are released from the Impact lead.

Tie a 45lb swivel to the end of a 30lb hooklength and run a section of 20lb line through the lower eye of the swivel. A hook is later tied at each end of the swivel to make the wishbone. A bait stop and a bead are added to the hook snoods on either side of the swivel before the hooks are tied on.

Stop knots can be made with a 1cm length of silicone tubing. Pass the hook snood line through the tubing twice and pull the line taut. Both hooks are clipped in position behind the Impact lead/Imp prior to casting. The length of the main hook snood between the swivel and the bait clip release on the Impact lead can be between 1ft and 4ft.

Adjustment for clipping down to the Impact lead is made by moving the Power Gum stop knot below the swivel up or down the rig body line until the hook snoods are taut. The tension spring retains tension to prevent the hooks releasing prematurely on the cast. If two bulky baits were clipped on the single release clip of the Impact lead they could tangle together and fail to release, or at least wobble and rotate during the cast, cutting down on distance. A more efficient system involves adding a Breakaway Cascade swivel to one end of the snood so that hooks can be staggered, as in the loop rig.

Top Tip – The wishbone and bomber rigs are prone to tangle in slack water conditions, and are more often used in a strong tide. Constructing snoods in various colours of mono makes then easier to untangle.

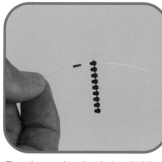

Cut the line at a sharp angle to aid the threading of beads, crimps, swivels etc. *Thread on a crimp, bead, rig swivel, bead and tension spring.*

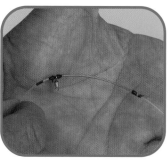

Secure with a crimp or Power Gum stop knot. *Tie on swivel to top of rig.*

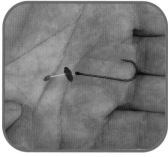

Measure the approximate rig length left and tie on lead link. *A length of snood line comes off the swivel and another swivel is tied to its free end. The hooklength passes through that swivel and a hook is tied on to it.*

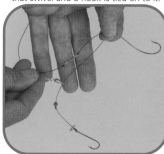

On the other end of the snood tie on a cascade swivel, and add another hook snood to that. *This allows the entire snood with a hook on each end to run through the swivel.*

By pulling the two hooks together they can be adjusted to fit the bait clips. *This allows one hook to sit behind the other.*

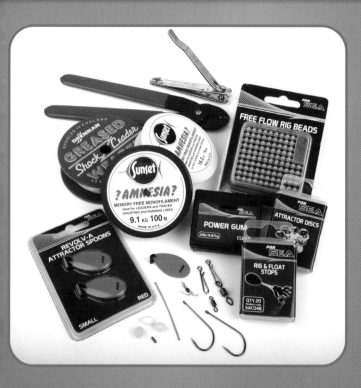

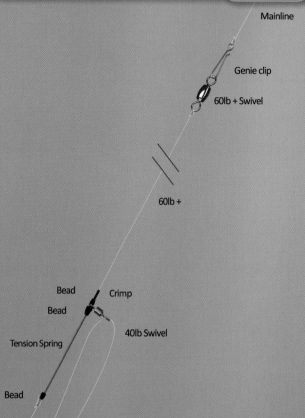

Mainline

Genie clip

60lb + Swivel

60lb +

Bead — Crimp
Bead
40lb Swivel

Tension Spring

Bead

30lb

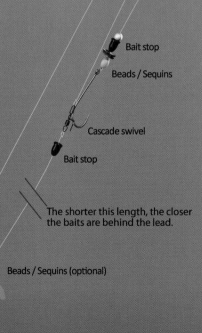

Bait stop

Beads / Sequins

Cascade swivel

Bait stop

The shorter this length, the closer
the baits are behind the lead.

Beads / Sequins (optional)

Impact lead

*"Blades, beads and sequins are
an option on the Wishbone rig
which is particularly popular
for plaice."*

BEADS, SEQUINS AND STOP KNOTS

Various types and sizes of beads are available for rig making, the most effective beads for this being the very tough micro beads. Buy cheap glass beads and they may well break, so beware. Streamlined, Aero beads are a favourite. Make sure your bead does not have a hole big enough for the crimp to go through – some makes have!

Beads for decorative purposes (to attract the attention of fish and bring them to your bait) are generally bigger. There are several types, including the latest floating beads which have proved popular and effective as a means to add buoyancy to baits and to lift them clear of nuisance shore crabs. All colours are available – in a survey of anglers it was found that yellow and white are the most successful.

Sequins are also popular as fish-attractors, especially for flatfish, and can double as efficient bait stops when used on the snood with a stop knot or a stop tube.
The latter is a 1cm section of Silicone tubing through which the snood line is passed twice. Pull the line tight and the tubing squeezes up to form the perfect stop knot to clamp the sequin or a bead into position. (see page 59)

OTHER RIGS

There are a number of alternative and specialist rigs used around the UK, and more – such as the weak link, split rig and bomber rig.

> *Top Tip - A big plus with a line clip is that in crossed line situations you can simply unclip the rig and keep it onshore, then retrieve the line, rather than dropping the rig back in and risking it snagging the pier wall or other obstructions.*

> *Top Tip - Tying a Genie link or a large swivel to the end of your reel line helps when threading the line through your rod rings. It also means you can clip a terminal rig on the end of your reel line with ease. This avoids the need to tie a knot every time you tackle up. All those extra knots will eventually shorten your leader.*

SPLIT RIG
Designed by England internationals this is an extra long terminal rig (20ft+) that is concertinered down to just 6ft so that it can be cast. The rig is used to fish for bottom and surface feeding species at the same time, using a float or floating beads on the top snood.

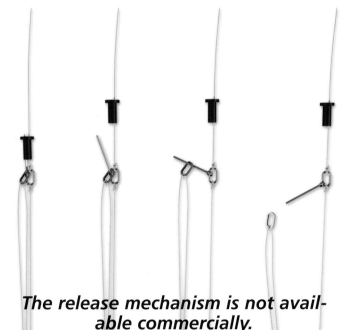

The release mechanism is not available commercially.

Stop Knot

The stop knot has various uses on terminal rigs and is generally tied using power gum or a light mono (15lb). Three or four turns are sufficient depending on the pressure on the knot.

1. Take a short length of power gum and lay it along the line.

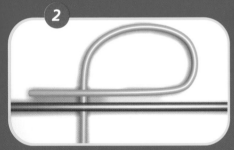

2. Take one end back on itself to form a loop.

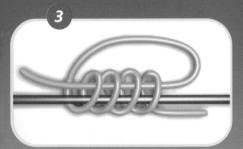

3. Take the tag end back through the loop three or four times.

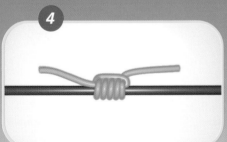

4. Moisten the knot with saliva as you pull it tight. Once the knot has been formed, with gentle pressure the knot can be moved along the line.

In some situations where the knot is likely to be moved regularly tie two knots, one in reserve.

There are three main knots used for rig-making in this book: the Grinner for tying swivels, clips and stop knots; the half-blood knot for all hooks and the sliding stop knot which is used some of the more advanced rigs and is covered on the previous pages.

Take great care with knots, because they are potentially the weakest link in your rig. Ensure that they are correctly tied and formed before pulling them tight, and do this gradually. Friction can damage even the largest-diameter mono, so tease the knot together carefully, moistening with saliva while doing so, especially if you add an extra turn to a Grinner for more security.

In the main a two turn Grinner knot is sufficient for heavy line above 60lb. Beware, though – some of the more supple leader lines can slip, and you may need to tie three or even four turns. For stop knots a three or four turn Grinner is sufficient. For hook knots a five turn half-blood is ideal for lines over 20lb. For lighter lines increase the number of turns, and for very light lines add a tuck.

Wetting a knot with saliva to help it form is common practice with large-diameter mono lines, but on some of the newer co-polymer lines wetting can actually result in increased friction, so check the type of line you are using before starting to tie up your rigs.

CASTING SHOCK LEADERS
The only other knots required for joining the heavy casting shock leader to the main line are the Bimini Twist and the Uni knot.

The Bimini (named after the Pacific island where it was used for big game trolling) is an extremely strong leader joint for lines of widely different diameters. Take time to learn how to tie this knot because it will save you tackle and fish.
The Uni Knot is simpler but not so strong, and therefore more suited to the casting field or clean shorelines.

A casting shock leader is a stronger length of line that is attached to your reel line to take the pressure of power casting with heavy leads. Casting leads over 4oz with lines of less than 30lb breaking strain is dangerous because the compression created by the rod will cause the lead to break the line. It is worth repeating the equation for calculating the breaking strain of the shock leader and rig line strength.

Multiply the weight of the lead or sinker by 10 – for example, a 6oz lead x 10 = 60lb shock leader; 7oz lead x 10 = 70lb shock leader and rig line.
Power or pendulum casters often add an extra 10lb for safety. Your leader needs to be the length of the rod, plus the drop to the rig and approximately eight turns around the reel spool. At all times, keep the leader knot away from your thumb – the Bimini, in particular, is a large knot that can do you damage when you fish with a multiplier.

Grinner Knot

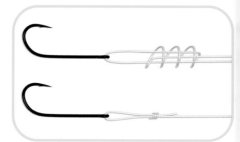

The grinner knot can be used to tie hooks, swivels etc and is the knot that is used on the bimini twist shock leader.

Uni Leader Knot

The easiest and quickest shock leader knot to tie is the Uni knot. Originally developed by tournament casters, this knot is small and unobtrusive but is not suited for rough ground.

Half Blood Knot

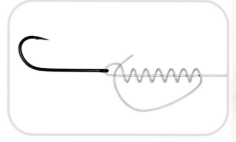

The half blood knot is favoured for tying hooks (minimum 5 turns). It does not leave a tag end on the hook eye that can trap the bait above the hook after casting like the grinner.

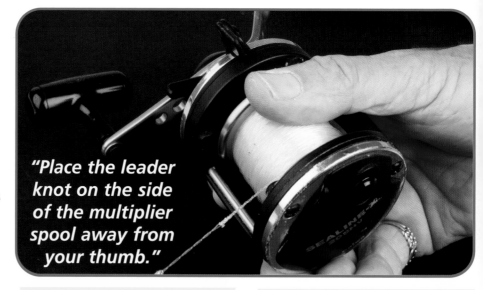

"Place the leader knot on the side of the multiplier spool away from your thumb."

Top Tip – When fishing from piers, high promenades or cliffs, use a longer casting shock leader. That way, when you lift a big fish, the leader knot will be on the spool so your lighter main line will not have to take the strain.

Top Tip – A textured finger cut from a rubber glove can be used to gain extra purchase on a multiplier spool and protect your thumb from the leader knot.

Bimini Twist Leader Knot

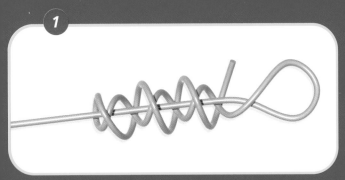

1. First find a place to anchor the loop. You can use a rod rest, door handle etc. Its essential to keep the loop under tension. Now form the loop and twist twenty times, more loops for lighter mono.

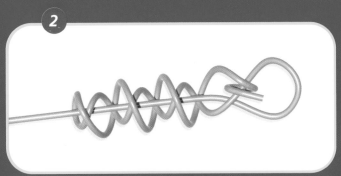

2. Lock the loop off with a half hitch around one leg of the loop.

3. Alternate half hitches on both legs of the loop, you can also tie a half hitch around both legs together.

4. The required number of half hitches to prevent the knot slipping is around six.

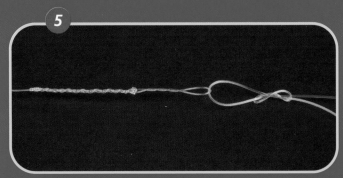

5. The shock leader is tied to the bimini loop via a two turn grinner knot.

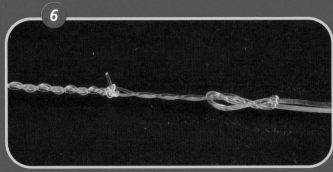

6. Once the grinner knot is tied in the loop pull it tight slowly and the knot will form and lock into the loop.

7. Trim lose ends of the knot with clippers and finish the knot by melting (blob) the mono ends with a lighter.

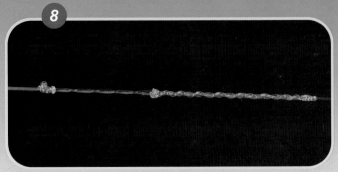

8. The finished knot.

Please take care with this stage. This procedure should not be attempted by children under the age of 16 unless supervised by an adult.

Leads or sinkers run between 1oz and 8oz for general sea angling. Check your rod's casting rating for the weight of lead it is best suited to.
The first type is the standard breakout lead for use in average tides. It has four grip wires that help hold it in the sea bed, but on retrieval the wires snap open so they no longer snag or bump along the bottom. In stronger tides anglers switch to a lead with four fixed wires which do not snap open. The third option is a plain lead, which can be used to allow baits to find their own destination in the tide. These, though, are not always practical because they tend to be swept inshore by the surf.

The turbulence of the surf and an onshore wind makes the choice of a lead very important, not only to gain casting distance, but to keep baits stationed where they are cast. In the main, 5oz is the best casting weight in terms of maximum distance for the average angler, and linked with grip wires it will hold in average conditions. Heavier leads from 6oz to 9oz can be used to punch baits through wind, sink tackle quickly in deep water and hold against a strong tide.

A range of different lead/sinker shapes are available, but in recent years casting distance has become the most important decider of sinker design.
Aerodynamic shapes like the bomb and torpedo have proved the most efficient and popular for beachcasting.

Tide and wind pressure on the line are what move the lead and terminal rig, and the further the cast, the more pressure is placed on the greater length of line in the water. This, in turn, potentially loosens the grip of the lead in the sea bed. Keeping your bait in position is one of the most important elements of UK shore angling, especially when the sea environment is hostile!

Top Tip - Multi purpose screw in head design sinkers like the Gemini range save the need to carry lots of different leads. You simply mix and match wire types to a range of body shapes and weights.

BREAKOUT LEAD

The most popular lead design is the original breakout (Breakaway) in torpedo and bomb shapes. These feature twin tensioned grip wires that snap open when the lead is retrieved, allowing it to be pulled over quite rough ground without the wires catching in the sea bed.
The more recent Impact lead is a breakout lead with built in fail-safe bait clip release system.

Impact Lead

Other lead patterns include the Gemini, which has a different single wire release system with optional screw-in heads, and various very efficient Breakaway/breakout copies available from local tackle dealers.

Gemini Flat Back

"The Gemini flat back lead (above) is used for extra grip on soft sand sea beds"

FIXED WIRE LEADS

Deep water piers and narrow estuaries, where tide and currents are strong, require a sinker that goes down quickly and offers maximum grip – a fixed wire pattern is perfect. They are more difficult to retrieve than breakout leads because the wire grips catch on the sea bed as they are pulled back, although because several grades of wire stiffness are available this need not be a problem.

Fixed Wire Impact

Best are the Gemini design, but bend the wires into a U shape to improve grip and the likelihood of escape from snags. Soft wires are great for escaping rocks and line snags or holding bottom in mud. Springy and stiff wires are more useful in extreme tide over sand, or in deep water.

Gemini Fixed Wire

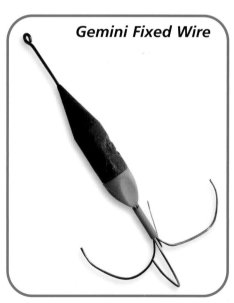

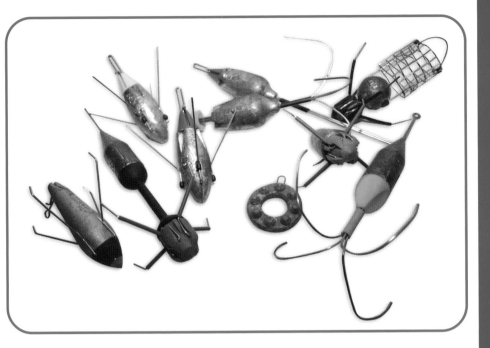

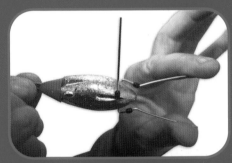

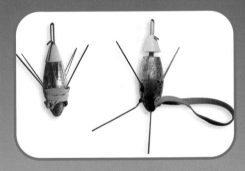

PLAIN LEADS

For fishing in less tidally influenced venues such as estuaries and harbours, or to allow the bait to roll or move with the current, a plain bomb-type lead down to 1oz and without grip wires is favourite. There are also a number of leads in various shapes that offer partial grip without the use of wires. These come in useful if the aim is to allow the bait to move downtide without fear of wires on the lead spooking fish.

Bomb, pear and torpedo: These are the most streamline shapes, suitable for casting and allowing a bait to trundle downtide.

Ball or sphere: This shape ought to be the favourite for casting, but it's not in common use at all.

Flat, spoon or lift: Grips the sea bed or skims up in the water, helping to avoid rocks and snags.

Watch, lighthouse, and pyramid: Old-fashioned shapes used to gain a grip in sand and mud.

New pimpled golf ball: The latest design from Italy for extra range, but does it work? I guess not. It may be a gimmick that never really took off.

Bullet or inline: This lead has a hole drilled through it. The line passes freely through this to lessen resistance to a taking fish. Perfect for float rigs or a running leger.

FEEDER LEADS

A recent development, feeder leads incorporate a wire or plastic cage or container to carry bait to the sea bed. They are generally used for medium range fishing and are obviously not very streamlined to cast. However, they are effective for match fishing, especially for the smaller species.

There is also the Intaki lead, with a sealed compartment which opens on contact with the sea bed to release the hook bait. This is used for casting delicate worm or mussel baits that might otherwise break up as they hit the water's surface.

Screw head: The Gemini lead type offers a range of different coloured screw-in heads with different wire configurations and weights (fixed and breakout) to cope with various tide strengths.

Long wires: The length of a grip wire determines its efficiency to some degree. Plastic tubing is used to support the wires so they can be bent away from the lead to add grip. Long, open U-shaped grip wires are easiest to spring out.

Long tail: A long tail wire is said to cast straight, rather like a dart, and that can be useful with large baits that tend to wobble when cast. A long tail also goes some way to averting tangles when a snood is used below the lead.

Impact: This is the latest Breakaway design with built-in bait clip that releases the hookbait on impact with the sea.

• Avoid soft, brass wire eyes which can damage, twist and break when fishing a rough sea bed. There are obvious dangers should a wire eye on a lead break. Grip wire length and springiness can affect efficiency. It's a good idea to check with a local tackle dealer what works best and is the most popular lead on a particular venue.

• You can adjust the tightness of a breakout wire by increasing the bend where it grips the lead. This enables you to match the grip and release tension to the sea bed you are fishing. In extremely strong tides, when closing the wires tight is not enough to grip, add an elastic band or small cable tie around the wires. You should also check and re-bend wires prior to every cast – this applies especially to fixed wires.

• The point where the line is knotted to the eye of the lead is a weak spot, so it's important to use a lead link to join the rig line to the lead and not to tie the lead directly to the line. A lead link allows the joint to move, and this keeps the knot clear of damage from rocks, stones etc during the retrieve. It also allows leads to be changed easily.

Countless hook patterns are the product of more than a century of sea angling. Hooks for species, hooks for bait, hooks for competition, beaked, offset, Kirby...the list is endless and confusing. In recent years the main hook companies like Mustad and Kamasan have concentrated on producing a more uniform selection. Fox are developing a range of hook patterns for UK conditions and species.

Anglers' preferences for hooks differ widely, and I would not question anyone's choice because confidence in your hooks is paramount. However, several design features are common to most of the favourite patterns.

Chemically etched hook points: These are the sharpest on the market because the hook itself is chemically coated, rather than being tumbled in a vat – an old-fashioned process that invariably dulled the point. The test for a chemical etched hook point is to run the point over your finger nail, it will stick in.

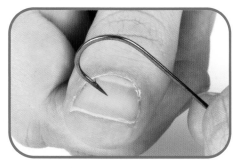

Carbon steel: Hooks made from this are light and strong, with small eyes that do not damage the bait as much as the over-large eyes of the past.

Aberdeen: The most popular and versatile eyed hook for sea fishing is without doubt the Aberdeen. It is a long shank pattern with a distinct squared-off round bend and small eye. Available in a host of wire types, strengths and colours from the different manufacturers, it is particularly favoured for use with worms and sandeels, because the long shank makes threading these baits on to the hook easier, and the small eye passes through the bait with little damage. The Aberdeen pattern is also easy to remove from fish, especially the small species and flatfish, because the long shank can be gripped and manoeuvred with the fingers more effectively than a short shank pattern. The Aberdeen is therefore the leading pattern for catch and release, being available in fine wire with a micro barb which causes fish little or no real damage.

Short shank: There are several medium and short shank hook patterns. These are usually preferred for baits like peeler crab, fish strip and squid baits, while very small short shank hooks are the choice for live prawns, sandeels and the like.

Spade end hooks: Popular in coarse fishing but not in universal use in the sea, although lots of match anglers have switched to them in the smaller sizes, so they should not be totally ignored.

Barbless hooks: Generally not practical in the sea. A micro barb is essential because of the line stretch and fishing distances involved. Without a barb, fish would be likely to slip or be washed off the hook.

Circle hooks: Practical for catch and release of a few species like tope, but for general shore fishing they are difficult to bait with worm, which rules them out of general use.

Bait barbs: Some patterns of hooks, often described as bait holders or worm hooks, have barbs sliced into the shank to secure the bait. These can have the effect of preventing the bait from reaching the hook point, so that fish grab a bait without the likelihood of being caught. Avoid bait holder hooks like the plague!

HOOK SIZE

The choice of hook size and pattern should be based on the size and type of bait being used and the size of fish sought. Beware of using a small hook in a large bait, because the bait will simply mask the hook point.

Hook sizes are standard. The smallest, from a tiny size 24 up to a size 8, are used almost exclusively by coarse anglers, after which the sea range starts. After size 8 the hooks get bigger up to a size 1. From that point an '0' is added – 1/0, 2/0, 3/0 up to 12/0. Sizes vary enormously between manufacturers, so beware of buying hooks without first seeing them. A general rule to remember is that a small hook can catch any size fish, whereas a big hook catches only big fish. You can use this to your advantage in several ways, but if you use a small hook to tar-

get big fish – by using a live prawn, for example – make sure you use a strong one. My favourites are the Fox Arma Point LS carp hooks.

HOOK SIZE/BAIT GUIDE

Size 6 up to size 2: Best for small flatfish like sole and flounder, plus mullet and garfish, or under difficult match conditions when fishing with small wriggly worms or fish strips.

Size 2 up to size 2/0: Generally regarded as the best all-round sizes for pleasure and match fishing from the beach or pier for all species with multiple small lugworm or ragworm baits.

Size 2/0, 3/0 and 4/0: Most suitable for large worm baits, sandeel, or cocktails of lug, squid and fish etc for cod, bass, ray and smoothhound.

Size 4/0 to 6/0: Large whole crabs, calamari squid, multi squid, live fish, mackerel head or cocktail baits for seriously big fish.

Size 6/0 upwards: Suitable for specimen conger, tope and all members of the shark family.

Hook Patterns

SOME FAVOURITE PATTERNS:

Varivas Match
Varivas Aberdeen
Varivas Big Mouth & Extra
Gamakatsu Aberdeen
Gamakatsu Reversed
Gamakatsu Aberdeen All Round
Gamakatsu Baitholder
VMC Aberdeen Fastgrip
VMC Aberdeen X Strong
Mustad Power
Mustad BLN
Mustad Viking
Hiro Aberdeen
Hiro Match
Eagle Claw baitholder
Arma Point Aberdeen MA
Arma Point Viking VK
Arma Point Bass BH
Arma Point Match FA

FOX FLEECES £49.99

RIPSTOP FLEECE LINED JACKET £24.99

FOX

RIPSTOP FLEECE LINED PULLOVER £24.99

FOX POLO SHIRTS £14.99

LOOK THE BUSINESS WITH FOX CLOTHING

FOX FLEECE
With British weather 'unpredictable' at best a fleece is essential at all times of year. This fully lined fleece jacket protects against the elements throughout the year, as well as ensuring you look the business when fishing too. It has an elasticated draw cord around the base and a secondary flap over the main zip to eliminate drafts making you cold. There are also two zipped outer pockets for storing smaller items like keys and phones. It's available in five sizes from small up to XXL. They sell for £49.99 each.

FOX RIPSTOP FLEECE JACKETS
If you're looking for a lightweight, warm and showerproof jacket then take a look at these. There are two Ripstop jackets in the range – a pullover plus a zip-up version – both featuring a hard-wearing, showerproof ripstop outer shell. This is combined with a fleeced lining with hand warmer pockets to make this the idea choice for cool summer evenings through to cold winter sessions. They are available in sizes from small to XXL and sell for just £24.99 each.

FOX SEA CAPS
Four smart caps make-up the Fox Sea headwear range. All feature the Fox Sea logo and sell for £4.99 each.

FOX POLO SHIRTS
The Fox range includes many hard-wearing, high-quality Polo Shirts, ideal for use when fishing or even when socialising. For up-to-date information on the latest colours and designs check-out the Fox website. Sizes available are small to XXL and expect to pay just £14.99 each.

ALL ITEMS OF FOX CLOTHING CAN BE PURCHASED ON-LINE AT www.foxint.com

Or, order direct on: 0208 559 6510/6511.
Have your credit card details to hand. Postage and packaging charges will apply.

CHAPTER 3
VENUES AND TACTICS

The marine environment is wild and untamed. Unlike coarse fisheries which are often tailored to comfortable and successful angling, the sea sees Mother Nature totally in control. Large expanses of sea are far more affected by the weather than rivers and lakes, and the sea angler has to overcome not only the natural caution of the fish species he pursues, but the hostile environment they live in.

No matter where you fish in the sea, the wind, tide, season, water depth and type of sea bed will all affect the likelihood of catching. Sea angling is one big learning curve, because no single standard technique is guaranteed to work at all venues or at any time of year.

Here we look at the basic tactics used on many of the different types of venues and conditions.

The most successful sea anglers will be able to adapt to local conditions and fish with an ever-open mind.

Fish like a robot and you may catch a few, but stay alert, be aware and you will learn something new about fishing on every trip and improve as you go along – remembering it all is the hard bit!

THE TIDE

One of the variables that has a major influence on sea angling success or failure is the tide. The seas around the world are influenced by the gravitational pull of the sun and the moon, and this produces a surge of water around the globe as the planets rotate. Water depth and speed is altered constantly by this tidal surge. Two high tides (flood) and two low tides (ebb) occur in every 24 hours, and these advance in time as the Earth spins and the position of the sun and moon changes. Because this is a consistent movement, tide times and heights can be predicted accurately and tide tables are made available years in advance. The shape of the land mass also has an influence on tide times and water depths because the sea is funnelled and directed around headlands and through narrow straits at many points around the coast.

The marine habitat and the behaviour of fish is greatly affected by tidal strength and water depth. In general, the more tidal movement there is, the more fish movement there will be. Peak tides on the ebb or flood produce the best results on most venues, but there are exceptions.

The shorter tides are called neaps, and they occur when the gravitational pull is at its weakest. The strongest, spring, tides occur when the combined gravitational pull of the sun and moon is at its maximum – the name 'spring' has nothing to do with the season.

The highest, strongest spring tides are universally recognised as being the best for shore fishing – but they are also the fiercest. Fishing can be quite difficult at such times.

The fish use the tide to travel to a food source, coming in on the flood and going back out on the ebb. The weather combines with the tide to produce food. For example, a strong onshore gale and heavy seas will dislodge and kill a lot of marine life. Fish instinctively know what conditions produce the most food, and will home in on it.

It is an easy matter to find out the precise times of high and low water, and the strength and height of each tide. Anglers who keep records will soon find that certain venues fish best under a quite precise set of conditions. Tide tables, available from most tackle shops, provide the basic information, and it is then up to the angler to interpret them from past experience.

Knowing the tide height and times are essential to the angler who digs his own bait, because spring high tides see the sea retreating the furthest, often exposing virgin sea bed which is a goldmine to the bait-digger.

BEATING THE TIDE

By far the biggest problem for the shore-based sea angler is keeping the tackle still on the sea bed in a strong tide. The more line in the water, the greater the pressure on the lead, and so wired grip leads are used to combat the strongest tidal movement. Breakout wires snap open when tackle is retrieved, making their recovery easier, but in extreme tidal conditions fixed grip wires are essential. There are other factors that come into play in holding your rig and baits in place on the sea bed, and certainly line diameter has a great effect. The larger the diameter of the line, the more it opposes the tide and the more it is likely to be dragged into a bow downtide. Lower diameter lines offering less resistance are most efficient with 0.35mm (15lb breaking strain) line, the standard for combating strong tide.

Casting slightly uptide to allow for the movement of the tide is acceptable, but take care not cast over another angler's line. Heavy leads sink the quickest, and are worth considering in deep water and strong tide.

Anglers can use the tide to move their rigs and bait in a positive way – floatfishing or freelining a bait are productive methods for some species, although many bottom feeding fish will not take a moving bait. Plain leads can be used in the same way as a float, to trot a bait downtide or allow it to move into a slack or eddy where food may also collect.

TIPS TO BEAT THE TIDE

- Adding rig tubing to the ends of grip wires assists grip in sand. Short wires grip better in mud, while long wires are easier to 'spring' out.
- The wires on breakout leads are adjustable, and can be loosened or squeezed tighter so that they grip and hold better – check and reset every cast.
- Once a lead is dislodged, especially when the breakout wires have come unclipped, tackle will be swept downtide. Retrieve, and reset the grip wires, or replace the lead with a more efficient size or pattern.

At the very heart of shore angling success is the ability to cast a bait out past the raging surf, and keep it there. For many, casting is a major stumbling block, so a later chapter will deal with the styles and techniques needed to attain greater distances.

For now, let's assume your casting skills are average – by that I mean you can cast a bait 100 yards with some regularity. Standard tackle for clear beachcasting is 12lb to 20lb lines and 6oz leads.

Most of the fish species found around our shores are caught by casting a baited terminal rig and sinker (or lead) as far out into the deeper water as possible, or with accuracy to features like sand banks, gulleys and rocky outcrops.

Specialised tackle and techniques are required for clean, mixed and rough ground, but in the main casting distance is achieved by having balanced tackle. This means a compatible rod and reel and a terminal rig that gets the bait out with the minimum resistance from the wind and tide.

When fishing over clean ground (sand, shingle or mud) it is generally the longest casts that bring the best results. Some species that swim close to the breakers, like bass, flounder and sole, can be caught with an accurate short cast, but in the main it is distance that matters, especially when the wind and tide conspire to make casting and keeping your gear in position as difficult as possible. The angler who learns to cast long always has the option of fishing short when conditions dictate.

Casting over medium or rough ground requires a strong outfit. Lines between 18lb and 30lb breaking strain are preferred, teamed with large-capacity reels to cope with the heavy line and strong rods needed to cast heavy leads, or drag tackle and fish from snags.

Results will depend on several factors, but predominantly the chosen venue and the time of year it is fished. There are no captive fish in the sea, so the seasons and the weather can present you with either a fish-packed venue or a fishless desert.

Because we cannot see under the surface of the sea, and have active imaginations, we will often fish when conditions are against us. Far better to seek out local knowledge – this can improve results enormously and is the biggest single advantage the sea angler can gain.

"Cast to the right spot and your catches will improve"

"At the heart of shore angling success is the ability to cast a bait out past the raging surf, and keep it there"

*"Remember water depth and
tidal strength effect where
your tackle ends up"*

TACKLE SNAGS

*When fishing a completely new venue, try mentally
mapping out the sea in front of you in a grid system. This is
especially effective over rough ground. Check out each grid
for snags and likely fish-holding spots. Don't just cast at
random, or back to the same spot if you lose tackle*

Try to find out about any venue before you fish there. Local clubs, tackle shops and newspaper angling reports are an excellent source of information. You should be able to find out about high and low tide times and strength (height), the best baits and times to fish, the type of sea bed, the best wind direction, and the effects the weather has on the fishing. You'll learn about what species to expect, and benefit from local knowledge – for example, if you intend fishing from a pier, is there is a landing net available?

It's best to check out a new venue over low water. The exposed sea bed will reveal the deepest and clearest ground to fish. Look for features, which can be obvious (a rocky outcrop or weedy reef) or more subtle (a change of depth in the sand). From a rocky or cliff mark, look for access to the sea, a safe place to land fish and, vitally important, your exit point on a flood tide. If you are fishing a remote venue, especially at night, never go alone.

When fishing a completely new venue, try mentally mapping out the sea in front of you in a grid system (left).
This is especially effective over rough ground. Check out each grid for snags and likely fish-holding spots. Don't just cast at random, and don't cast back to the same spot if you lose tackle – only if you get a bite.

Top Tips
• To remove weed from the line without having to put the rod down and stop reeling, hit the side of your rod with your palm sharply several times. This will clear the obstruction and allow you to carry on retrieving.

• A stable aluminium tripod with a sliding butt cup is a positive aid to keeping your rod safe in a rough, weedy sea because it can be used to raise your rod tip high above the surf, thus preventing weed and swell from pulling the lead free, or the rod over. Avoid small tip rings when fishing a weedy sea because these will jam with a weeded leader knot.

• If you arrive at a new venue at high water it's a good idea to cast a plain lead where you are intending to fish and then retrieve it slowly. This can reveal any contours, ridges and rocks.

• Take care when reeling in large clumps of weed, and do not put the strain directly on the reel. Lift the rod, pulling the weed in, and then reel as you lower the rod to take up the slack. This is known as 'pumping' and is an easy way to retrieve heavy weights. An alternative is to walk backwards and then reel in as you move forwards.

• Line diameter has a big effect on your casting range and the control of tackle in wind and tide. A low-diameter line will oppose tide and wind less than a heavier one. A line diameter between 0.30mm (12lb) and 0.38mm (18lb) is reckoned to be the most effective for clean beach fishing at long range. If choosing braid, use a line of the same breaking strain as you would mono. This is a far finer diameter (0.06mm), and explains why braid casts particularly well when used on a fixed-spool reel.

"A good beachcaster will be able to cast past the surf regularly"

"A big plus point of an estuary is the shelter it offers in all weathers"

Lots of sea angling venues are affected by river estuaries. The ever-changing mix of fresh and salt water leads to the kind of marine environment only a few species can fully exploit – these include flounder, eel and mullet.
The more distant the beach is from the river mouth, the less it is affected by the freshwater coming down in times of flood, heavy rain or snow melt.
Among the species commonly found in these outer estuaries are bass, ray and stingray. Depending on the size of the river, codling, coalfish and plaice may also be present.

The inner estuary and the lower reaches of many of the larger rivers are the ideal choice of venue in spring and summer, when fish move inshore in search of the vulnerable peeling (moulting) shore crabs. Many such places offer comfortable promenades to fish from, and easy access.

You don't need specialist tackle for the estuary. A normal 15lb line-type beachcaster will suffice, although a lighter 10/12lb line and a rod casting 2oz to 3oz can be more fun higher up the river.

Often a snippet of information can point you to an estuary hotspot, although a low tide reconnaissance is always worthwhile. On most estuaries this is easy, because they empty of water over low tide – but take care not to get cut off as the tide floods back. Most of the large estuary venues fish best from low tide through to the first hour or so of the flooding tide. Favourite routes taken by fish tend to take in weed-covered rocks, ledges, sand banks and gullies.

Fish know that every low tide the crabs will shuffle stations, and so the first up the estuary with the flood tide will invariably find the most food. This raises an important point about estuary fishing – the action is often short-lived and determined by the state of the tide. The fish move through, often in shoals, feeding as they go. You have some hectic sport for an hour or so, and then they are gone again.

You are not necessarily guaranteed action on the ebb tide as they return to the open sea, because often their route is via channels in mid-estuary, or even skirting the far bank, which may be miles away!

Picking a spot from which to ambush the fish as they move up the estuary is not difficult, because your low water reconnaissance will have revealed places to which you can cast a bait. However, it's no use picking a comfortable place to push in your rod rest if it means you have few features to cast to. In any event, most times you will need to move with the tide as it floods, and this makes accurate casting even more difficult.

You can learn about hotspots from the locals, but that's no reason not to search for your own ambush points. Remember, these will change with the tide, so the more mobile you can be, the better results you are likely to achieve.

Casting accuracy is crirtical in an estuary because the fish will be nosing in with the tide and it's easy to overcast them.

Don't leave your bait out too long. Not only may it be removed by the local crab population, but it may be outside the fish's route upriver as the tide comes in.

Top Tip - Coarse angling brolly attachments work equally well fitted to the back rest support of a seat box. They are ideal for brolly security when fishing from promenades or pier walls, for example.
You can use coarse fishing bait trays in exactly the same way.

Nothing is worse when you are fishing than losing tackle. Not only is it costly, it's time-consuming too, sometimes costing you fish as well. But worst of all, it can affect your choice of venue. Many sea anglers, especially beginners, avoid some of the best fishing venues there are, just because they have a reputation for being snaggy.

Yet fish love the selfsame snags that cause us grief. The major survivors of the commercial nets are the species that live in the thickest, densest cover – rocks, kelp, even angler-generated snags of lost tackle.

All are home to a population of fish simply because they offer shelter and food. Fishing amid snags of any kind does require a degree of common sense as well as the correct tackle. All the snag-beating devices in the world will not compensate for a poor technique, and that's often the real reason anglers steer away from rough ground – they, or their tackle (or both) cannot handle it.

The first step to saving tackle when fishing amid snags is the correct rod and reel set-up. Your rod should be powerful enough to lift your rig and lead off the bottom and bully the fish up and over kelp or rocks without folding – soft rods and rough terrain do not go well together.

A well loaded, fast retrieve reel is also essential. Modern fixed-spool reels offer the speediest retrieve because they have a large-diameter spool. However, many anglers feel that the multiplier is more practical and comfortable to use over the rough stuff.

Whatever you chose, ensure your reel is well loaded with line so it retrieves to its full capability. One thing to know about a multiplier is that after your rig has been cast, its spool diameter is reduced dramatically. This means less line per turn of the handle is put back on to the spool at the vital start of the retrieve.

Fixed-spool reels are better in this respect because the spool diameter does not reduce so much after casting. If you use a multiplier, retrieve as fast as you possibly can initially to clear the sea bed. Then, once the spool fills and the lead is off the bottom, you can slow the retrieve rate.

Whatever terminal rig and lead you choose, ensure that you lift the lead off the sea bed and start retrieving all in the same movement, and don't stop reeling until your gear is clear of snags. A slow, dragging retrieve over the sea bed can lead to tackle snagging, as can stopping to feel if you have a fish on. Don't do it, otherwise your fish may become hooked up on an obstruction and lost.

Line breaking strain is another major consideration. Light lines of around 12lb to 20lb may cast further, but they require a shock leader, and this is a potential weak spot if your rig snags. If you pull for a break you'll lose both rig and shock leader. Seasoned rough ground anglers prefer to use 25lb to 35lb line all through. Casting distance is restricted, but by using a lighter breaking strain snood and a weak link, snagged tackle can often be retrieved. If you need to use a lighter line for distance, don't go below 18lb and use the strongest of leader knots, such as the Bimini twist. Remember, too, that the further you cast over rough ground, the greater the odds of snagging!

There are a variety of accessories and devices to help you avoid or escape from the snags. These are all optional add-ons to your rig.

"Rough ground is a sanctuary for lots of species including the rarer ones like this trigger fish"

"Rocky coasts, although productive for fish because the trawlers cannot get to them, can be very dangerous"

Lead lift: A plastic vane that is clipped above the lead to help it plane upwards towards the surface. These work well on many venues, but on others do no more than help add to the end rigs potential to snag, so use carefully.

Planing lead: Many regular rock anglers use lead designs that are flattened or shaped to make them rise in the water and these are a better alternative to the lead lift. You can even flatten a bomb lead to help it plane towards the surface. Alternatively on some venues a fixed wire lead can help the lead grip in and prevent it falling into crevices etc.

Weak link/rock release devices:
These are the most effective way to retrieve tackle and fish from the roughest terrain, however the devices all rely on the lead being lost if it snags and so can prove expensive. A good idea is to use either cheap moulded leads or old worn out leads.

The variety of lead release accessories include several purpose made rock releases from the manufacturers as well as several home made designs. A favourite home made device is a panel pin with a small piece of polystyrene glued to it. This allows the pin to float out of a loop holding the lead on the lead, bringing the weak link into play. Others include a wire which holds the lead but is released by a disc as the rig hits the surface. Others have a weak link device that doesn't require a weak link of line and include a disc system which releases the lead to a wire prong set to a "weak" pressure you can adjust. The simplest system of all is a wire link that the lead is hung on, the link

in turn hangs on the clip on the rig. The lead comes off on impact with the sea, there is a version of this link with a built in bait clip.

Most of these weak link devices work by releasing the lead once it hits the water or sea bed. The lead is left tied to a short length of light monofilament line (6lb to 15lb) that can then be broken free easily if the lead becomes snagged.

What breaking strain mono you use as the "weak link" can be very important. On extremely snaggy venues a 6lb mono link will allow a very easy "break" and retrieve, whilst 15lb will allow the angler to try to pull the lead free with the weak link.

In all cases a weak link device will not have any effect on rig retrieval if the hook or top clip of the rig is snagged - it only works for the lead.

A word of warning, if you are power casting, the weak link devices that do not support the lead fully and come adrift during the cast pose a potential danger and should only be used for short range and overhead casting.

ESCAPE TIPS
- Having lost a rig consider a move, simply shifting the angle of your line by moving down or up the beach a few yards can make all the difference with small tackle snags whilst terrain snags can often be overcome by reducing hook number and casting further. Whatever, it is foolish to throw rig after rig at a tackle snag without attempting to avoid it somehow.

- Make a mental picture of the sea bed you are fishing over, often a snag can be avoided simply by casting down tide, longer or shorter. Avoid casting uptide in strong tide on a snaggy beach - You are simply allowing your lead and rig to travel further down tide increasing the odds of catching a snag because it will end up slightly down tide anyway.

- Line snags are a particular problem on many beaches and it's the right angled wire of breakout grip leads like the Breakaway and Gemini that gets caught in the lost line. This cannot break out and inevitably leads to line breakage and loss of the rig. Using a soft fixed wire grip lead and you can escape line snags as long as you bend the grip wires in a U. Avoid fixed stiff wire grip leads with wires bent at acute angles!

- The final action to escape a snag involves pulling for a break. Never try to break out of a snag with the rod tip, especially jerking it hard, this could break the tip. When you feel you have tried pulling steadily from an angle, pulling from high up and all the other methods to escape a snag there is nothing for it but to point the rod at the snag, clamp the line around the butt and walk slowly backwards until something gives. Sometimes you will be lucky, sometimes you will lose the terminal rig and leader.

- Carry a spare reel loaded with 30lb line straight through if you are fishing a strange venue. This will allow you to beat the snags in the worst conditions. Nothing is worse that arriving on a venue and discovering that 15lb mainline and a small reel is not tough enough to beat the snags!!!!!

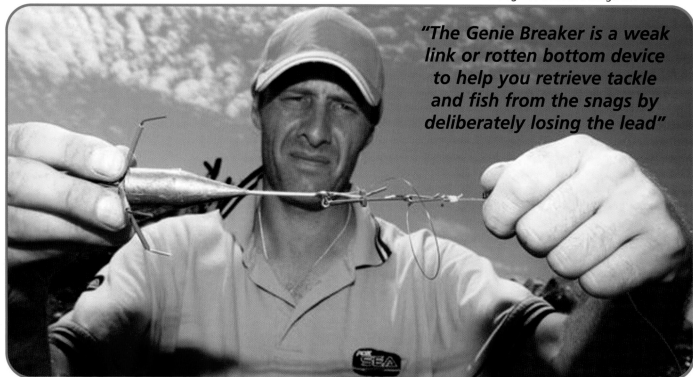

"The Genie Breaker is a weak link or rotten bottom device to help you retrieve tackle and fish from the snags by deliberately losing the lead"

"Want to know what the sea bed looks like when fishing from rocky coast? Look behind you, the undersea rocks usually mirror those of the cliffs"

"Piers and breakwaters offer access to deep water and a host of different species"

"Some form of rest prevents rods sliding off railings"

The pier is an obvious attraction to sea anglers because it offers easy access to deep water. There's no need to cast far, and generally there are lots more fish on offer than direct from the beach. All this has made the piers increasingly popular with beginners, and in peak holiday times they can be crowded places. But, as autumn looms, the holiday feathering hordes leave the piers to proper sea anglers and very often a seasonal Indian Summer weather pattern offers mild and settled conditions before winter proper arrives.
Don't miss it!

There are two types of pier – walled and stilted – and both provide a complex habitat and a food supply for a large mix of sea species. The pier is like a mini reef with shelter, weed growth and nourishment attracting marine animals and fish. It's a complete marine environment in what would otherwise be, in some cases, a flat, featureless sea bed.

Fishing from a pier requires a wide spectrum of angling knowledge and skills. It's the most complex branch of sea angling to attempt, which is why many novices – drawn to the obvious attractions of the pier – struggle to cope with the many problems they then encounter.

The biggest challenge can be the strong tide. Walled piers, in particular, oppose the tide, which increases in strength where it meets the wall. Stilted piers allow the current to flow under them, so the tide is not so strong, but there is the ever-present danger of tackle snagging and tangling on the structure.

Both types of pier have fish-holding areas alongside the walls or piles, on the sea bed in the immediate vicinity, or near the surface under weed and cross beams.

A range of tackle and tactics is required for the pier, but none of this will be of much use if the wrong species are targeted at the wrong time of year – techniques are very seasonal as fish come and go.

A major attraction of most piers is that there is always water to cast into, but the fish found under and around the pier are at their most active at certain states of the tide. Most piers fish best during the flood or ebb tide run, others yield their best results during a series of spring tides, and still more required a neap tide to perform well. Finding the most suitable tide to fish is part of the local knowledge of pier fishing, and if a favourable tide happens to coincide with dusk or dawn, that is when catches are likely to peak. Fish feed well in low light conditions.

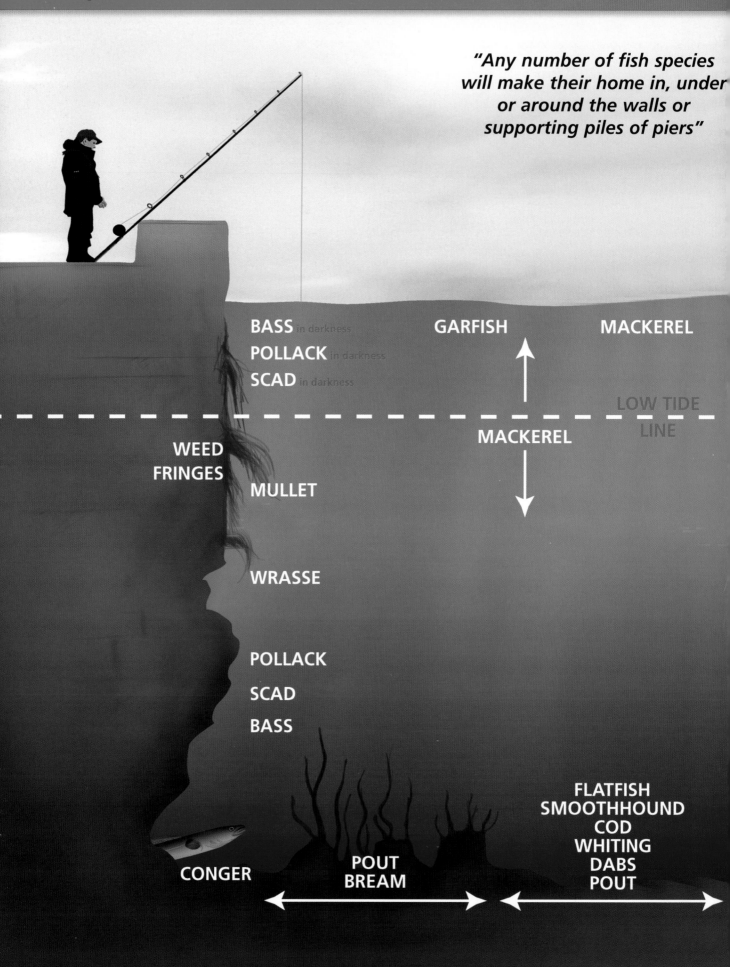

"Any number of fish species will make their home in, under or around the walls or supporting piles of piers"

BASS in darkness
POLLACK in darkness
SCAD in darkness

GARFISH

MACKEREL

LOW TIDE LINE

MACKEREL

WEED FRINGES

MULLET

WRASSE

POLLACK

SCAD

BASS

FLATFISH
SMOOTHHOUND
COD
WHITING
DABS
POUT

CONGER

POUT
BREAM

The end of the pier attracts lots of novice anglers. They reason, usually wrongly, is that the further out they cast, the deeper the water will be and the more fish it will be home to. You will catch a lot more than these people by giving due consideration to recent results from the pier and any fish-holding features it may have.

Lots of walled piers produce back eddies in the current which collect food and draw fish to them like a magnet. Some walled piers have holes or weed-fringed overhangs where fish take up residence or shelter. Fallen debris from the wall can also create a haven, while fish will always be drawn to where anglers gut their catch and throw away any unused bait. The most reliable way to find the hotspots is to ask, although in many cases the throng of anglers gives the spot away.

Pier fishing does not require specialist tackle, and a 12/13ft beachcasting outfit rated for leads of 4-6oz will be suitable for most situations.

Lighter, specialist rods may be required where overhead casting is banned, for boom hanging, or for float rigs. In these situations light mono or braid lines may be used, but in general a beachcaster and a reel suitable for 15lb mono line, plus shock leader, is all you need to start with.

Terminal tackle essentials include fixed wired grip leads in 5oz and 8oz for combating the tide, especially on walled piers, where the strength of the current is amplified by the wall. Other things you will need are some means of securing your rod to a wall or railings, and access to a landing net (usually a drop net on a rope) for getting big fish up on to the deck of the pier.

TOP TIPS FOR PIER ANGLERS

- The proximity of other anglers on a pier brings the inevitable line tangles, but on the plus side it's a great place to learn about sea angling, and often the friendly banter and camaraderie is a major attraction in itself. Piers have their own angling clubs, well worth joining if you want to fish regularly.

- The pier is one of the few places that allows groundbait to be used effectively. A strong mesh bag filled with bread, boiled mashed fish like mackerel, pilchard oil and other additives can be lowered into the water to attract a range of fish species.

- Good advice when fishing a stilted pier is to always fish on the side of the pier stem that faces into the tide. The tide then forces baits on to the sea bed, rather than up off the deck.

- When resting the rod on a railing or wall, position it well above the mid balance point to prevent it being pulled over by a biting fish or rubbish hitting the line. The rings can be used to help keep the rod stable and in position, or angled to suit bite spotting. Pier and railing rod rests are available.

"Down the wall is the hotspot on most piers"

"Not all bass caught on lures are giants, but catching a bass – any bass – on a lure is an achievement"

Spinning or plugging for bass is a growth area in modern sea angling. The rise in the number of protected nursery areas for bass has increased school bass numbers, new sewage and water treatment plants around the coast have improved water quality and clarity, and the many new coastal protection rock groynes have added accessible venues and created favourable conditions to fish for bass.

Bass aren't the only species to take a lure. Wrasse sometimes go for them, as do garfish, coalfish, scad and mullet, but spinning and plugging is mostly to do with bass, pollack and mackerel.

The suitable tackle set-up includes an 11ft spinning rod that will cast up to 60 grams and handle lines from 10-15lb. Look for a sea spinning rod, rather than one aimed at freshwater species such as pike and perch. In general a sea spinning rod offers that extra poke to handle large lures, snags, and the wind and surf. A fixed-spool reel is first choice, again a model suitable for casting 10/15lb line.

The terms 'spinning' and 'plugging' reflect the type of lure being used. In many cases predators are chasing small fish like sandeel, sprats and herring, or even the smallest fry, and a range of lures are suitable to replicate these. Spinners, being metal, are usually heavier and more aerodynamic than plugs. They are favoured in situations where the baitfish are being driven by shoaling predators, often mackerel and bass. In their frenzy, and being in competition with others, bass often become less wary of the lure and will grab it without paying much attention to its appearance or the way it moves. The heavier metal spinners cast further and sink quicker, and it is important to control the depth at which they fish, with a fast and aware retrieve.

Plugs are made from plastic and various bulky and less aerodynamic materials, but their movement when retrieved is far more fish-like than a basic metal spinner, and they prove more effective for less competitive fish or lone specimens, especially bass. Many of the best fish lookalike plugs and lures include a diving vane on the nose. The angle and length of the vane determines the depth the lure dives to – the faster the retrieve, the steeper and deeper the dive.

Others float, and the vane makes them dive on the retrieve. These are particularly favoured for fishing rough ground amid

boulders or weed. A jointed body may give the lure a very lifelike wiggle!

The latest lures are the soft rubber and synthetic shads and similar fish-shaped lures. Many of these have a flexible rear end and fish-shaped tail for a realistic movement when retrieved. These sit somewhere between a spinner and a plug.

For bass, the first essential is to find a productive venue. Bass are members of the perch family, a shoaling species renowned for their their patrolling instinct. Find one bass and you will find more, but they are not common everywhere so you need to know the venues they are caught from. In general, look for vantage points where you can cast a lure to bass. Because casting range is not great with a lure, this means headlands or rocky outcrops. Coastal protection rock groynes are excellent because the water rushing between and over the boulders surfs and fizzes, conditions young bass love. Flat, open beaches are not always the best places to fish, although wading to reach deeper water ledges and reefs is a tactic worth considering, and one that is successful for those seeking to catch bass on a fly.

Once you have found your venue, the next step is to maximise its potential by covering lots of sea with your lure. Being very mobile by carrying very little tackle allows the angler to continually keep on the move. A small sling bag, rucksack, bum bag or even a trout-type body warmer with lots of pockets is quite suitable. The trick is not to have to put anything down when you start to fish. Even a net can be dispensed with – that way you can be continually on the move.

Footwear is important. For rock-hopping, a stout pair of waterproof boots gives support to the ankles, whereas an old pair of trainers is okay for the younger and more agile angler. Chest waders are suitable for wading, but in the warmth of summer these can prove a burden.

Casting range with a lure is restricted by its shape and weight. The old favourite jointed plug patterns have severe limitations, but more and more modern weighted – though still buoyant – lures are becoming available. These cast further and can be retrieved slowly, therefore for longer. This means that the fish has more time to spot and take a lure.

Another breakthrough in respect of casting distance is the use of micro braid lines. Thinner than conventional mono, these cast further and more smoothly. Not only that, braid lacks stretch, which brings other advantages. These include a more positive strike and a feel for the lure that is transmitted to the rod top, enabling the angler to skim over snags. On the downside, a lure hooked up on braid is difficult to free. A compromise might be the use of a mono shock leader.

Bass, like many other species caught on lures, will shy away from anything continually cast and retrieved over their heads. This is why, when boat fishing for bass, the boat is usually drifted over the fish rather than anchored up. It's the same from the shore. There are many places where bass can be caught consistently, but even these fish will grow wary if you stay in the same place for hours – so leave the hotspots to rest and make a note to return to them on your way back along the beach.

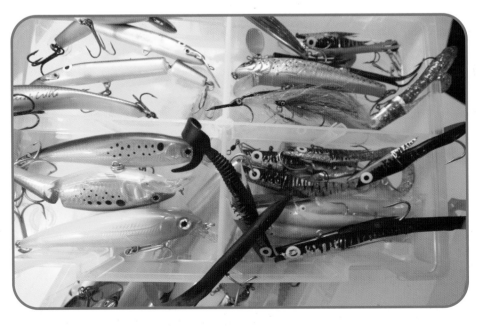

THE RETRIEVE

Different retrieves suit different species. Pollack will seldom go for a lure that is jerked in a 'stop-go' manner, maybe because they feed on sandeels that swim fast and straight. Bass, on the other hand, will take a lure that swims erratically and fast, an action resembling that of an injured fish. So will mackerel. Jointed, diving plugs are deadly for both species.

When a floating plug with a nose vane is being reeled in, speeding up and slowing down the retrieve, even stopping it, causes the diving lure to rise to the surface. This way the angler can cover a large area of the water column as well as a good distance! One consistently deadly tactic is to retrieve right up to the point where the lure hits the rod tip. Bass are notorious for taking the lure at the last second, just before you lift it from the water, so dip the rod tip in the sea and retrieve the lure to it.

Wary bass will also follow a lure for some time, even striking at it from the side and front rather than the rear, not something that most anglers are aware happens. Once fish have grown wary, a change of lure sometimes works, but far better is a move away to less spooked fish!

THE LURES

Changing the lure is an important tactic. We all have our favourite pattern, but being able to change the colour, action or size of the lure instantly can improve casting distance and the chances of a take. A small American snap link tied to the end of the line allows lures to be changed in seconds.

Many plugs and lures incorporate two or sometimes three sets of treble hooks, but removing one or more of these makes the lure less prone to hook-ups when you are fishing around rock and weed.

The selection of a lure is often a matter of personal choice, not all those used by sea anglers were intended for bass in the first place. For instance, I regularly catch bass on a rainbow trout pattern. Mackerel-striped patterns and colours are by far the favourites, though not necessarily in their natural colours. Hot red and orange, and especially red and white, seem to be very successful combinations.

Other lure features include vibrating devices and even an internal rattle. These help catch species worldwide in murky water, which might explain why bass are caught here in less than ideal conditions.

Poppers are surface lures that splash and skitter on the surface. They are deadly and exciting lures to fish with worldwide, and many UK anglers use them regularly, but they are considered best when bass are shoaling up and feeding avidly.

TIPS WITH LURES

- Retrieving a lure shallow or near the surface is often the best option because it can be seen easily by the fish, silhouetted against the surface. A deeply fished lure may be hidden by the background.
- Want to experiment with braid line? Use a softer rod for braid because its lack of stretch can be abrupt, whereas a softer rod can help cushion takes and a fighting fish.
- Absolutely the best tactic for catching bass on a lure is to fish as dawn breaks or dusk arrives. Make the effort, you will not be disappointed!!
- Don't be put off by silly lure names. Lots designed for the tropics catch bass.
  - Always buy your lures in twos – nothing is more infuriating than losing a deadly lure that is catching fish and not having another to replace it!
- From the shore, bass will rarely take a lure that has a lead weight in front of it, so always use a pattern that is heavy enough to cast in its own right.

"Dusk or dawn are the hot times for spinning and plugging"

As the sunlight fades, fish move inshore from the deeper water to feed. Both large and small fish are instinctively secure in the dark water, and marine life in general is more active. Darkness is a time when the sea angler's chances of success are multiplied, and even the greenest novice is likely to catch. If you have never considered or tried fishing at night, then you may be missing out on some of the best and most exciting sea angling around. Success is not always guaranteed, but it's highly likely that the numbers of fish within YOUR casting range will be massively increased.

Night is not without its problems, though, not least the blackness of a desolate or remote beach. The sea shore at night can be an eerie and sometime dangerous place. Anglers tend to band together, and most productive night venues are fairly crowded, especially at weekends. So if you are nervous of the night there are plenty of places to fish among other anglers – even well-lit promenades and piers. But if you are fearless, the night offers a multitude of fishing opportunities to get your hookbait close to some big fish. That said, fishing with a pal is generally considered a safe and sensible option, even for those with an adventurous streak. Brave anglers are likely to fish the more remote and dangerous marks, and the potential hazards are fairly obvious.

Night fishing has its hot periods, and at most venues the best times to fish are between 8pm and 3am, with high water before midnight. For a few early-rising species like sole, bass and ray the hours before dawn can be deadly, but in general two hours either side of midnight is the time to expect cod, whiting, pout, dog-fish, conger and many others. A few species seldom feed in the dark. These include wrasse, plaice, mullet and mackerel.

"Good lighting and creature comforts make for better concentration on the fishing"

Calm, clear nights are generally more productive than when the sea is rough and coloured, because fish often feed close to shore in daylight in such conditions anyway. In calm, gin-clear water, fish are more active in darkness, but a full moon can be as much of a deterrent as the sun to fish coming inshore on some shallow venues.

There are few hard and fast rules, but the generalisations mentioned usually apply. Tide times can make all the difference between success and failure.

When selecting a place to fish at night, first check it over in daylight, ideally at low tide to reveal the layout of the sea bed. You can avoid snags, check out the casting distances to prominent features and, very importantly, check access to the mark and how safe it appears. Turning up on a strange venue in darkness is fraught with dangers, especially on long low water venues, rock marks and cliffs. Make sure you are aware of your exit point(s), and ensure your chosen fishing spot is not subject to sudden swells.

Most night anglers prefer to fish venues where there is only a short distance between high and low tide marks. These allow you to have a base and do away with the need to continually move with the tide. Where you actually set up base camp can greatly affect your fishing, so pick your spot with care. Take into account the tidal direction and strength, remember the flood and the ebb will run in opposite directions, and stay downtide of groynes or other obstructions that your tackle may be swept into. Your base camp needs to be back from the high tide mark. Check out the beach ridges, or the position of the flotsam on the last tide line, and take into account the fact that neap tides will be dropping back while spring tides will move further up the beach. Remember that a building wind may push the sea in further at high tide than you expect!

A base camp in the form of a Beachbuddy, a similar shelter or even a basic umbrella is essential for night fishing. It keeps your gear and bait dry, it is somewhere to retreat to, and it centres your angling world. Position it just back from the beach ridge, allowing room for your rods to sit on a rod rest to the front or side. Add a fuel lantern and you have an oasis of comfort that can make even the coldest, dampest of nights enjoyable to fish in. Most beach anglers rely on a head lamp for activity outside the base camp, and an increasing number use electric base lamps as well. Dual halogen, LED headlamps offer a light spread and a beam option, and are powered by the latest lightweight, long-life niCad batteries.

BASE CAMP LAYOUT

A compact and well organised base from which to fish, day or night – especially on the beach – prevents gear being lost and allows vital tackle to be placed near at hand, ready for when it's needed. Take special care with bait, which is susceptible to the weather. Rain and a chilling wind will kill worms. Your bait also needs to be organised away from clumsy feet. Don't lay your complete supply out to face the elements, just unwrap as much as you need for a few casts.

Having spare terminal rigs to hand is essential at night. These can be pre-baited to save time between casts, and should be positioned safely out of the way. Most of the rod rests you can buy today have rig bars and rig clips, and these are ideal.

Spare reels are a must in case of an overrun, tangle or line loss to a snag. Nothing is worse than having to untangle or reload a reel on the beach – lost fishing time always coincides with when the fish start biting with a vengeance!

If you use a fuel lantern then it will benefit from being raised off the ground. If you are not superstitious, an upturned bucket does the job, but a pole is better – and the higher you position the lamp, the bigger its pool of light will be.

Towards the back of the shelter, spare clothing will be kept dry and food and drinks will be at hand.

There are lots of small items you can easily lose in the dark. Bait cotton is always going walkabout, so it's a good idea to have a spare supply. Keeping it in a tube helps. Similarly knife, scissors, baiting needles and line clippers are easy to bury in the beach. A Fox lidded box for such items solves that problem!

Headlight

NIGHT FISHING TIPS

- Lots of novice anglers find it difficult to cast during darkness because they cannot tell when their lead has hit the sea. The answer is to switch to a fixed-spool reel, which cannot overrun. An alternative is to load your multiplier with less line, and tighten up the magnetic/brake spool control. There is not always the need to cast to the horizon in darkness. Practice is essential – try a venue with lights to help your confidence before going into the pitch blackness.

- A Starlite whipped to the rod tip with bait elastic is ideal for spotting bites. Alternatively, paint your rod tip white. The typewriter corrector fluid Tipp-ex is ideal. Wrap a tapered strip of reflective tape around the Tipp-ex – problem solved.

- Beware of placing your rod tip too high, or watching it will give you a stiff neck. Position the tip at eye level, where it is comfortable to watch. A double rod rest with a spare rod also helps spot variations in tip movement and is handy in a wind.

- For umbrellas, the perfect solution is one of the freshwater brolly attachments which fits a seat back rest. Alternatively, strap the brolly to your box with a luggage strap and pile stones on the edge. For shelters you can use beach stones or water in a couple of buckets or plastic bags, but remember to dispose of them properly when you leave. Cable ties and short luggage elastics all keep shelters stable by enabling them to be attached to fences, railings or groynes.

- Boredom can cause night anglers to drift off during marathon sessions when big-fish tactics produce little action. Use a second rod and fish with a multi-hook rig for the smaller species. This will keep you alert, and guarantees a catch to take home. Small-fish and crab activity can be a vital clue to big-fish behaviour on lots of night venues. If your bait is vanishing in seconds, it's a good bet that there are no large predators around, whereas you may notice a drop in crab activity when the bigger fish show up.

- Keep an eye on the sea on calm nights. Bass, in particular, often come very close, taking discarded small fish off the surface – it's worth trying a livebait if you see a swirl!

"A relative of the marlin – if only garfish grew to 10lb!"

Most of the species caught around the UK feed hard on the sea bed, but many fish that visit our shores in summer are pelagic. This means they swim and feed off the bottom in mid-water or near the surface. Garfish, mackerel, pollack, mullet, bass, bream and wrasse are just a few of the species that can be caught off the bottom on float tackle. There is something magical about watching a float bobbing along in the tide and then suddenly disappearing. It's a fishing method to try before you die!

The sliding float system is favourite and most effective because it allows you to alter the depth the bait is fished at in an instant to suit the tide or species. A stop knot made from monofilament line (lighter than the main line) or Power Gum tied on the mainline (four-turn Grinner knot) above the float can be slid up or down the line to adjust the depth at which the bait is fished, remembering that the tide is forever on the move and so the water will be getting deeper or shallower. Two stop knots are a good idea if you are making lots of adjustments, because with use they can wear out and come adrift.

With the bait off the sea bed, the float can be allowed to drift in the tide, searching out the immediate area. A large float can also be used to prevent large and powerful pollack or wrasse from crash diving back into rocks and weed.

Top Tip – A bubble or casting float is the answer to catching garfish at long range. Use a fixed float and mono paternoster with long snoods, and size 8 hooks baited with fish strip.

In most situations, float fishing involves using a single hook. More than one hook can be used, although this does increase the chances of the rig tangling during the cast.

Rods and reels are generally quite light to suit this type of fishing, with lines of 8-12lb. A carp rod would be ideal, but beachcasters are not suitable.

OTHER TACTICS – STRIKING

Striking allows the angler to get totally involved in the capture of his fish – like squeezing the trigger of a gun, it's angling's crucial moment. However, striking may not always be as important as it might appear, because lots of sea fish hook themselves. We all like to think that driving the hook home is crucial to success, but does it make that much difference to the success rate, and are there different ways of striking for different species?

The fact is that some fish will rarely be hooked if you do not strike at the precise moment they take the bait. These are usually species that are caught in clear water, or that are aware of the hook, line and sinker. Coarse fish are a classic example, having learned to avoid hooks because they have been caught and returned to the water. At sea this problem is not so acute, but there are a few sensitive species – the mullet is one – that will only occasionally hook themselves. However, many other sea fish will hang themselves even if you don't strike, simply because they are intent on eating the bait and oblivious to the angler!

The way a particular species feeds, what it eats, its mouth structure and its mobility...all these factors determine the ease or difficulty of hooking it.

Most of the speedy tropical mid-water predators are less easy to hook than the bottom-grubbers such as the flatfish. With some species, like flatfish, once the hook has entered the mouth it cannot escape. Others, with large, bony mouths, are difficult to hook because the hook cannot find a place to stick!

Those more lethargic species with time to circle the bait, bite it and take it down most often hook themselves, and a deliberate strike makes little difference to the catch rate – although it does massage the ego of the captor to think so. However, a premature strike has more influence in preventing deep-hooking!

Overall, for fishing around the UK, a less enthusiastic approach to striking will result in more fish being hooked. The decision on when to strike depends on what the angler wants from his sport, what he is fishing for, the type of bait being used and how keen he is on conservation. If the rod is lurching seawards and is in danger of being lost, then a strike is essential. If the rod tip is nodding continuously it's likely that the fish is already hooked.

The actually strike can vary from a full-blooded sweep of the rod to just a tightening of the line. Line stretch at distance, of course, reduces the amount of movement at the hook end of your tackle, and some anglers even run backwards during the process of striking to increase that movement. Reeling as you strike can also prove effective, but beware of striking too hard, especially at short range, when it may test your tackle and knots. Can anything beat feeling a fish pulling the rod tip down hard, striking, and seeing the rod bent double? I doubt it, but missing a few fish is a fact of life and something all anglers have to live with, so don't take striking too seriously. It is not an exact science by any means!

COD: A relatively slow bottom-grubber with a large mouth, a cod invariably swallows the hook when left to eat a dead bait on the sea bed. Powerful rod-pulling bites generally occur only after the fish has hooked itself. Slack-liners from codling can be most difficult to hook, and the answer to these is patience. Take up the spare line and only strike when the fish pulls the rod tip down hard.

WHITING: The devil's own job to hook on occasions, easy on others, this predator attacks baits in numbers, with some tremendous rod-pulling bites that are easily missed, especially in a slack tide. More fish are hooked when fishing in strong tide, because the fish have to swim to stay still to eat the bait. When it is engulfed, they relax, and the tide drives them back on to the hook. Short snoods and neat (small) bait presentations can improve the hooking rate.

BASS: A fast-feeding predator that rarely swallows the hook because the bites are so positive. Be close to your rod when this fish takes off. It has a bony mouth, so a large, sharp hook is essential.

"World champion Chris Clark pulls the trigger on a big wrasse from Kent's Samphire Hoe"

DAB, SOLE, PLAICE and FLOUNDER:
Often flatfish peck and nibble at the bait but invariably, once they engulf the bait, they are hooked because their mouth is far smaller closed than open. There is in fact no way to prevent flatties from swallowing the hook, and hook removal is often fatal, even with soft wire hooks. For the conservation-minded, tiny hooks (size 8 and under) can be removed with less damage than large ones.

SMOOTHHOUND AND TOPE: Positive bites give the angler every opportunity to pull the trigger on these species, which is why they are so popular and such fun to catch. The tope is one of the few UK sea species that circle hooks are really suitable for, but there is a definite technique for striking with circle hooks and it involves a steady tightening of the line, not a full blooded strike!

RAY: Invariably this species flops on to the bait, causing the rod tip to tremble. Later the fish moves off, having taken the bait, pulling the tip down, slackening the line or sometimes pulling the rod over. Because of the way they feed, ray are often foul-hooked outside the mouth by a premature strike.

BLACK BREAM: These are among the most difficult sea fish to hook because of their bait pecking and small mouths. Use light line and small hooks, keep bait size down, fish carefully and be patient.

GREY MULLET: Mullet, like many coarse fish, will shy away from large hooks and thick line. Bites are often positive but need to be struck, as the fish will expel hook and bait if they feel resistance. Only the thin-lipped mullet is suicidal. One essential rule when fishing for thick-lipped greys is, never strike by sight. When you see a fish take the bait, always wait until the float disappears or the tip goes round!

DOGFISH: This is perhaps one of the most difficult sea fish to hook, but catch rates can be improved using frozen sandeel on a size 1 Aberdeen. Patience is essential – don't move the rod or bait once you've spotted a bite.

CONGER: The old school reckon a conger should be given time to take the bait, but this may allow it to swallow the hook, so striking early is recommended.

TIPS ON STRIKING
- Holding your rod and gripping the line between the fingers, you will be able to feel the tugs from the small species, and it's a fun way to fish. Experiment with striking and you will find that in the majority of cases catch rates are greatly improved by letting the fish bite for a few seconds before hitting it. Of course, when using multi-hook rigs to catch fish for the pot, letting the fish hook themselves is far superior to striking at every rod tip rattle!

- If you are going to strike, ensure that the reel is not in freespool mode or on the ratchet, and that you have a firm footing. More than one angler has struck at a screaming ratchet and fallen flat on his backside.

- Patience is a virtue, they say, and more fish will be landed if you take your time and do not rush at the strike. Let the fish take the bait, and strike early only if you intend to release your catch.

- Braid line and its lack of stretch allows for more positive bite detection and striking. However, your rod needs to be softer to compensate when a powerful fish is hooked.

- Bait size and presentation are very important in relation to when you strike. Use a single lugworm on a size 2 hook and you can strike fairly quickly, but with a double squid on a 6/0 Pennell rig you may need to give the fish longer to get into the bait. Also ensure that baits do not mask one another. There is no need to hide your hook in the bait.

- A major problem for lots of sea anglers is that they allow baits to grow too big by continually adding fresh worms to washed out worms, for example. Baiting fresh and paying attention to presentation every cast will invariably result in an improved strike and catch rate.

Finally – if in doubt, hang on a few seconds before striking. Sit on your hands if you have to!

GROUNDBAITING
Although groundbait is not commonly used by sea anglers, it is effective in some situations and becoming more and more a consideration. A bread bag is the common tactic for attracting mullet, pollack, bream, garfish, mackerel and scad to a float fished or freelined bait from many piers and rock marks. The simplest bread bag is a net bag (a sprout bag from the supermarket or a laundry mess bag) on a rope. This is filled with a mixture of boiled fish and bread or bran, and hung from the pier wall or a pier pile. You can add pilchard oil, or a tin of sardines or pilchards, for an oily slick which works particularly well for garfish and mackerel.

You can use the same groundbait mixture to improve your chances from piers and rocks, although this type of feeding proves less effective anywhere that has a very strong tide. Scatter or spoon the contents on the rocks during the rising tide for a constant groundbait slick.

The alternative is a feeder, and a number of larger sea versions of the coarse fishing feeder are available. Fill these with chopped fish, shellfish, catfood, coarse pellets, sweet corn, the list is endless. A little imagination is needed, but the method has its merits.

Boat anglers have refined the bait dropper system for wreck fishing, and this is another device that anglers may benefit from using from a pier, or any marks where casting is not essential.

TOP TIPS

VENUES & TACTICS

- Vary your casting distance to find fish on a strange venue. Often fish follow the edges of sandbanks, gullies and the gutter found at the low tide mark on many venues, can be a real fish concentration spot. Groynes are also a super hot spot because in nearly all cases fish have to swim around the end to pass them and casting accurately can pay big dividends.

- Want to cast a small lure or bait a long way so that it retains buoyancy and moves with the current or tide? A bubble float part filled with water for extra weight is great for lures and bait, both on the surface and sub surface!

- Fishing over really rough ground can be hard on tackle, but there are ways to reduce the risk of tackle loss. One that is not commonly used is to use a softer wire hook. Of course, the hook strength needs to be able to cope with the fish you seek but that does not mean using a hook capable of pulling a bus ashore. Softer hooks can still catch fish and at the same time help you escape the rocks.

Arma Point Viking VK

- Fish are more difficult to hook in slack tide so give bites longer to develop. In a strong tide the fish are having to swim to maintain their position level with the bait and once they take it are pushed back in the tide and this often sets the hook.

- Lots of anglers have a fascination with big fish and this means that it's the big fish that are most likely killed, whilst the tiddlers are returned. In truth more damage is done to fish stocks by the killing of a large breeding size fish - why not take a picture of your capture and then release it? Take the tiddlers to eat, they are much tastier.

TACKLE

- Ever thought about using coloured beads to identify different rigs in your rig wallet? Ideas like black beads for single hook rigs, red for multi hooks. Orange can be used to signify a snood below the lead or green for a particular design.

- Walking a long way to your fishing spot and wanting to save weight inevitably means leaving something behind. Better to take essential gear but balance it up for carrying. A rucksack or tackle box with a carry harness makes a big difference and adding a few heavy items to a bucket spreads the load.

- There is nothing worse than finding yourself without something to wipe your smelly hands on. Fish rags have far more going for them than many anglers think. Old tea towels, hand towels and bath towels cut in squares are ideal. Lay a spare one in the base of your tackle box for emergencies. Another tip is to wrap your spare reels in hand towels and these can also be used as fish rags if needed.

- Carbon spigot joints can jam on a hot day as carbon expands. If your rod joint is really stuck try cooling it with a frozen ice pack, or under the freezer lid. After a few minutes, when the temperature is lowered, the joint should part easier.

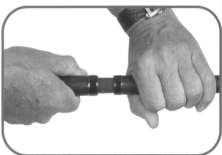

- Loose ends of line spooling from your multiplier or fixed spool reel can be a reel pain inside your tackle box. Use a short length of PVC tape to tape the line down or for the fixed spool a Velcro rod band or elastic band can work.

- The line clips on most of the sea fixed spools are not designed for shock leader line and it's a devil's own job getting the line under them. Solve the problem by keeping the line in place with your finger stool elastic. Haven't got a finger stool for casting? Get one, they are an absolute boon to keeping your finger safe and undamaged by the leader knot when casting and using the elastic on it to retain the line on your reel spool and you won't lose it!

- Carry one of the light weight LED headlamps in your tackle box as an emergency back up. They are getting better and better. Only one essential though, replace the batteries with the longer lasting alkaline type.

- Want a trolley for the pier or promenade? check out the freshwater types with pneumatic tyres. The crude, heavy, old fashioned models often sold for sea angling maybe cheap, but they are noisy, hard to pull and go rusty quick.

CHAPTER 4
SPECIES

UK waters offer a diverse range of fish species. Some are resident, some migratory, some are bottom dwellers, others pelagic (swimming near the surface). We even have some sub-tropical visitors. Many have suffered from commercial exploitation, leading to depleted numbers and a smaller average size. Others (usually prey fish) have thrived because of the demise of the exploited species, while some newcomers have arrived either as the result of a more plentiful or untapped food supply, or because of global warming.

Sea angling success can vary, depending upon where you live and fish. It is also affected by water temperature – there is a southern and a northern migration pattern of summer and winter species throughout the year. However, recent warm, prolonged summers have meant that many of the southern species now range much further north, and their season extends longer.

One thing that has not changed is that the catching of sea fish requires effort on the part of the angler. The 'chuck it and chance it' approach of the past is most inappropriate today.

Nowadays a bigger emphasis is placed on finding the fish, and with travel so easy many successful sea anglers follow the peaks of species through the seasons.

FISH GROUPS

The families of fishes found around the UK are divided into several groups – flatfish, rays, sharks, gurnard, eels, ling, codfish, wrasse, bream, mullet, mackerel, scad, garfish and bass. There are several other species groups among the smaller fish – mini-species – which are not always direct angling targets, but sometimes serve as bait. Among them are dragonets, pogges, weevers, gobies, blennies, rockling, herrings and sandeels.

SEASONAL MOVEMENTS

The movement and migration of fish has a great effect on results and we are constantly reminded about being in the right place at the right time. Cast where there are no fish and you go biteless.

The seasons have a major influence on fish movement, and we describe some species as summer fish and others as winter fish. When these two overlap, the result can be a fish bonanza.

Generally this is during the autumn, as early as September or as late as December. Global warming and the change in seasonal temperatures has an effect, while the arrival of the winter, which is always a gradual north to south progression around our coasts, means that some regions will fish better for longer than others, and at different times of year.

The main seasons and species around the British Isles are:

April, May: Spring sees the common shore crabs start to peel around many parts of the UK coast and this attracts bass, eels, pouting, flounder, codling, plaice, ray, dogfish, smoothhound and others inshore. After the rigours of spawning, many of these are hungry.

June and July: Summer arrives in the south of the UK with species like tope, smoothhound, ray, mackerel, garfish, scad, pollack, bass, mullet, gurnard, bream, plaice and sole continuing to arrive and spreading north. The baitfish – sprats, sandeel, mackerel and scad – are shadowed by many of the larger predators as they move north.

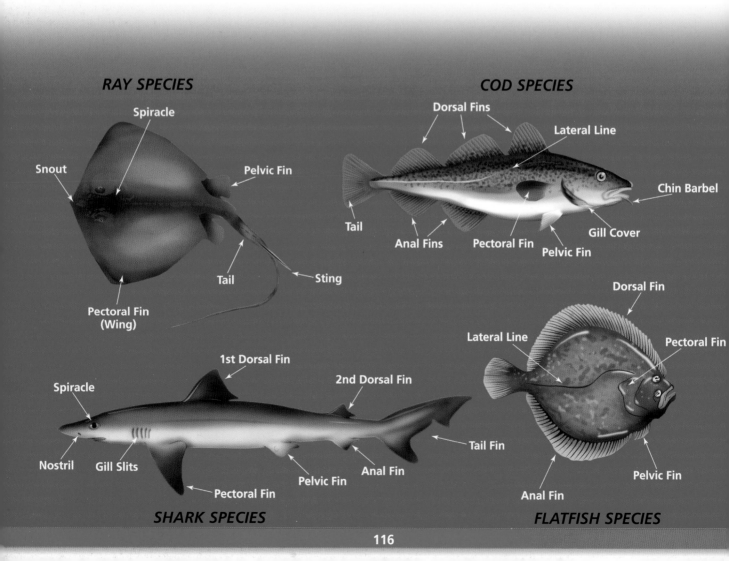

RAY SPECIES

Spiracle
Snout
Pelvic Fin
Pectoral Fin (Wing)
Tail
Sting

COD SPECIES

Dorsal Fins
Lateral Line
Chin Barbel
Tail
Anal Fins
Pectoral Fin
Pelvic Fin
Gill Cover

SHARK SPECIES

1st Dorsal Fin
2nd Dorsal Fin
Spiracle
Tail Fin
Nostril
Gill Slits
Anal Fin
Pelvic Fin
Pectoral Fin

FLATFISH SPECIES

Dorsal Fin
Pectoral Fin
Lateral Line
Pelvic Fin
Anal Fin

"Cod are the most popular sea species, with most shore-caught fish this average size...around 5lb"

On the west coast of the British Isles the Gulf Stream speeds the species surge north, while on the east coast the cold North Sea slows the northern migration. July is a month for the unusual – some of the rarer breams, rays, trigger fish and wrasses.

August: This can be a month when some species bypass venues in the far south – everything has moved north – but regional temperatures and sunshine can have an effect. Further north, August can be one of the best months of the summer for mackerel.

September and October: Usually a time of plenty in many regions, with the summer species like bass, mullet and ray having reached their maximum range and starting to overlap the resident and winter species like cod, whiting, pouting and dabs. The mix can produce some spectacular results, and this time is the best in most regions for specimen fish. It's also when most of the unusual or rare species extend their range furthest.

November and December: A time when the bigger bass and the bigger cod feed inshore on their way to their winter spawning grounds. Both take advantage of the carnage of the winter gales moving closer to shore. Generally bass start to move south, cod north at the end of this period, although in some regions both species move back into deep water. Seasonal cycles of species like cod produce an overlap of fish inshore when food is short and hungry mouths many. Lean cod years will see a shortage of bigger fish.

The weather changes in many regions at this time, and sea anglers have to be able to cope with low temperatures, wind and rain. The rewards for lasting the course are the bigger fish! Lots of whiting, dabs and codling will keep the rod nodding in most regions.

February and March: The slowest time of year in many regions. The bigger fish will have moved away from the shoreline to spawn, and only immature fish and a few localised species like flounder remain.

SPECIES LOCATION
Many common species have a liking for a particular marine location – it could be a specific sea feature like a reef, gulley, rock face or estuary. Here is a general overview of what species are found where.

Remember, though, that migration can place species in venues they are passing through, which is why this is a guide rather than a hard-and-fast rule.

Cod: Have a liking for deep water and strong tide which they use to travel to feed. They are found over clean and mixed ground, but can become localised among rocks and reefs, where they take on the colour of the kelp – so-called 'red' cod.

Bass: Small school bass are caught in estuaries and from surf beaches, especially when a large surf is running – then they often feed inside the main breaker. The bigger fish hunt around reefs and piers, especially in the shadows of harbour lights, and in fast tidal runs or anywhere easy food is available. Many piers where anglers gut mackerel and throw the entrails in the sea are home to some big bass.

Pollack: These are found on or off the sea bed behind pier piles, under weed fringes or close to pier walls, cliff edges, reefs or the edge of the tide flow.

Mullet: Active near the surface in calm water marinas and harbours, they can sometimes be spotted under boats, or around wind-blown flotsam. Find them feeding on the outer sea side of piers and they will be less timid.

Mackerel and garfish: Both species prefer clear water. The mackerel shoal up against rocks, pier walls and beaches, chasing small fish, where swooping gulls often betray their presence. Garfish, small relatives of the mighty marlin, are surface feeders, sometimes seen leaping around floating weed

Wrasse: Often located up off the sea bed around rock edges, pier piles or weed fringes. They are very localised in shoals – find one and there will be others. If you don't get a bite, move. Wrasse don't feed at night.

Conger: They can be very localised to a particular area of rock, holes in pier walls, the bases of cliffs or patches of rough ground. Nocturnal, they often venture out of their lair under cover of darkness to feed.

Sole: A nocturnal species, they are found on shell grit beaches, feeding in the last hours of darkness, or in coloured water, often very close to the shore.

Plaice: They prefer a sandy, shell grit bottom, anywhere near pea mussel beds, and sandy patches between rocks and weed.

Dabs and whiting: Found over clean, sandy, shell grit sea beds, they like coloured water best in daylight, clear water after dark.

Flounder and eels: Both are fish of the estuaries, but are also found on beaches on the edge of estuaries.

THE EFFECTS OF WEATHER ON SPECIES
A major factor affecting shore fishing results is the weather, with wind direction and sea temperature both having a major influence on occasions.
Generally a strong onshore wind produces a stirred and coloured sea, sometimes resulting in a sand bar or reef being gouged apart by the waves. The resulting marine carnage spills and kills lots of marine life, which obviously attracts the predators. A calm, clear sea with wind off the land still produces fish, but is generally best fished after dark, when fish are more active and far bolder. Rough, coloured seas in daylight are always more productive for the majority of species.

Some wind directions are better than others. An east wind is rarely productive countrywide, and in many regions, if it lasts for any appreciable time, it kills sport completely. A touch of north to an east wind is most productive on North Sea coasts. Alternatively, around much of the south and west coast, any wind from the west or south is productive.

Low winter temperatures can also affect how a venue fishes. A low tide mark exposed to heavy frost overnight can rapidly cool the shallow water and send fish packing. Floods and snow water have the same effect. As a general rule, in winter fish only shorelines where you are casting on to a sea bed that is never exposed over low tide.

"(right) A quick reference guide to when the main UK species are most likely to be caught"

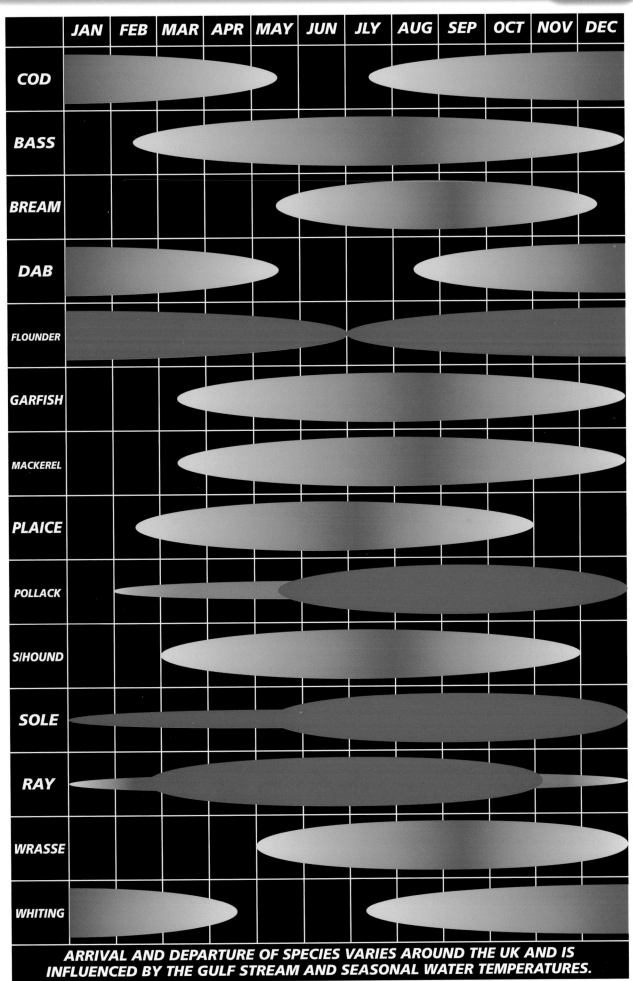

	JAN	FEB	MAR	APR	MAY	JUN	JLY	AUG	SEP	OCT	NOV	DEC
COD												
BASS												
BREAM												
DAB												
FLOUNDER												
GARFISH												
MACKEREL												
PLAICE												
POLLACK												
S/HOUND												
SOLE												
RAY												
WRASSE												
WHITING												

ARRIVAL AND DEPARTURE OF SPECIES VARIES AROUND THE UK AND IS INFLUENCED BY THE GULF STREAM AND SEASONAL WATER TEMPERATURES.

Not all sea fish are monster specimens, in fact the majority weigh less than 1lb. However, the chance of a large specimen of a few species is what keeps lots of anglers fishing. Here we look at the major species that reach specimen size.

COD (Family Gadidae)

A strong contender for the title of 'most popular sea species' the cod (Gadus morhua) is the largest of the cod family, and because it is also a popular fish for the table it has been commercially exploited to near extinction in recent years. Considered a winter species, with a mainly northern distribution, there are a number of large shoals that are found around the UK. The best cod fishing is found where these overlap.

The cod is a large bottom-feeding predator with a bucket-sized mouth, and can top 100lb in the northern parts of the Northern North Sea (ironically, in the sovereign waters of those countries that do not belong to the EC). Around the UK any fish over 20lb is considered a specimen, with fish half that size an excellent catch from the shore.

Cod are fast growing, nearly doubling their size annually during their first few years. Starting their life as codling (cod under 5lb), they can survive inshore on a mix of marine worms, crabs and shellfish before eventually moving into deeper water to concentrate on a fish diet as their appetite increases.

Cod are prolific breeders, and a large adult female can spawn up to six million eggs. These drift in the surface water layers and mature. In certain sea and weather conditions, usually during very cold winters, a large percentage of the eggs survive to become small cod, while in others they are wiped out by prey fish like mackerel and herring. This leads to a 'boom and bust' cycle of breeding years, but it explains the reason the cod survive, despite their over-exploitation commercially.

ID: The cod's large mouth and belly are major identification points, but it has three dorsal and two anal fins, a chin barbel and a white lateral line, with a light green pattern on the flanks.

BASS (Family Percichthyidae)

The addition of the word 'sea' to bass is something that gets under some sea anglers' skins. It's a culinary marketing ploy that gives the bass (Dicentrachus labrax) an element of class in a society that worships celebrity. In the heirarchy of the sea, the silvery, sleek lines and bristling image of the bass have a cult following among anglers. Members of the perch family, noted for their territorial, patrolling nature, bass can be caught regularly in the same haunts. They love the surf and are seldom found far from the shore. This is a major reason why the bigger bass are often caught by novice casters, and sometimes as a result of a short cast because of a reel overrun! Bass are shoal fish which are very slow growing, reaching breeding maturity only after four years or so. This has led to a considerable decline in fish numbers through commercial exploitation, although in recent years the introduction of nursery areas has aided a bass revival. The bass is primarily a warm water species, moving north around the UK in spring and summer and retreating south as winter arrives. Large bass appear solitary, but this is simply because, as a bass grows bigger and older, the odds of survival are lessened. One large fish may be all that's left of the original shoal.

Two strains of bass are known – the lower Atlantic or Mediterranean fish are shorter and stockier than the northern race.

ID: Major bass identification points are its silver, scaled flanks and large spiky dorsal fin. Only the mullet looks similar, but that has large rubbery lips. Beware the razor sharp edges to the bass's gill covers.

POLLACK (Pollachius pollachius)

The pollack is another member of the cod family with a liking for deep water when mature. That's why it is mainly small pollack the shore angler encounters – the bigger fish are found in only the most remote and rugged rocky locations close to deep water. A sight feeder with large eyes, the pollack is found in midwater and off the sea bed, feeding close to the surface in darkness. It has a liking for small fish, crustaceans and marine worms.

ID: Golden green flanks, large eyes, protruding lower jaw and a curved lateral line. Sometimes confused with coalfish, which is a close relative with similar behavioural patterns, but the coalfish has equal jaws and a straight lateral line.

RAY (Families Rajidae, Torpedinidae and Dasyatidae)

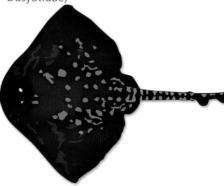

The ray family has made a big comeback in terms of numbers and size in recent years. Perhaps they have benefited from a drop in the demand for their flesh – they are labour-extensive to skin and pack – or it could simply be that the food left unexploited after the demise of the cod has allowed them to thrive. Whatever the answer, their numbers are on the increase.

There are several different species of ray and they grow to a range of sizes. The most common species are the thornback, (Raja clavata) and the small-eyed (Raja microcellata, sometimes called painted ray). Other rarer species include the undulate (Raja undulata), homlyn, cuckoo, spotted and blonde.
Here I am concentrating on the thornback and small-eyed rays.
They can be caught together, although in general the small-eyed has a southerly distribution and the thornback, the bigger fish, is found all around the UK. Although often described as a flatfish, the ray is not a relative of the flatties, but is a close relative of the cartilaginous species like the sharks. The rays are bottom-dwellers, and their underslung mouth and wide wing span are the ideal ambush combination. The ray will fall on small fish and your bait, and first bites are often a small twitch of the rod tip. Once the bait is taken the ray moves off, and bites are always rod-benders. Strike too soon and the ray is often hooked in the nose or outside the mouth.

Not renowned as strong fighters, rays

glide and kite in the tide and have been likened to a Tesco plastic bag, although that is perhaps unfair.

The thornback, as its name suggests carries an extensive array of thorns (watch your fingers) and the thorny scales can cut you when the ray is lifted. The ray has hard bony plates like the smoothhound – no teeth, but again watch your fingers. These are for crushing crabs and shellfish.

ID: Identification of some of the ray species can be confusing. The thornback is the most distinct. Most rays have some prickles, but the large broad-based spines of the thornback are distinct. The small-eyed or painted ray (Raja microcellata) has wavy streaks and blotches, while the undulate ray, which it is sometimes confused with because this is also called 'painted ray' in some regions, has streaks that are edged in white dots.

"Thornback ray numbers have increased in recent years"

"The smoothhound, a powerful mini shark, has extended its range around the UK and is one of summer's most popular shore species"

STING RAY (Dasyatis pastinaca)

The biggest of the shore rays, the sting ray, as its name suggests, has a venomous spine halfway up its tail – some have a double spine. Occasionally they are caught with their tail or spine removed by commercial fishermen. A spring migrator, the stinger moves north around the UK from April through summer, but does not reach the northern extremes of the UK. It prefers clean, sandy bottoms and is not found at all venues. Famous hotspots are Lepe and Pagham, in the English Channel, and St Osyth's on the East Anglian coast. The sting ray is the largest ray the shore angler is likely to encounter and although it is relatively rare, fish of 50lb-plus are landed every summer.

ID: Whip-like tail with barbed spine, rounded fins and no dorsal fins.

SMOOTHHOUND (Mustelus mustelus) & STARRY SMOOTHHOUND (Mustelus asterias)

There are two species of smoothhound, common and starry, although they can only be separated biologically and this relates to how they bear their young. Here we will talk about smoothhound as one species. Smoothhound range inshore from spring onwards in the south, moving north during the summer. They can now be caught as far north as Scotland. Some very big females are landed from beaches where the fish are inshore to give birth and to feed. Venues are often specific, with fish showing annually in some areas and not in others. The species has seen an increase in its numbers, size and distribution in recent years, and this may be partly due to the smoothhound taking advantage of a gap in the food chain. Anglers are adopting catch and release for the species, and to prepare the fish for market is labour-intensive. Catch and release is standard, and the smoothhound

is a species held in high regard for its power. An extremely strong fighter, it has a preference for peeler and hermit crab baits, but will also take fish, worm and squid.

ID: Smoothhound lack teeth. Instead they have bony plates to crush crabs and shellfish. They have two large, equal-sized dorsal fins, and both members of the family have the starry spots. The spurdog and tope are similar looking species, but the spurdog has bony spines in front of its dorsal fins and no anal fin, while the tope has an anal fin and sharp teeth.

CONGER (Conger conger)

The largest eel found around the UK, it frequents rough ground, reefs, wrecks, and piers. It is very strong, with powerful jaws and teeth that can rub through thin mono line. Nocturnal feeders, conger often only leave their lair under cover of darkness. Their ability to swim or squirm backwards with their tail around weed or rock demands extremely strong tackle. Any conger much above 20lb is a specimen from the shore, while the smaller eels, or 'strap conger', are more common from southern, south-western and western rock marks. They are no so common around the North Sea coasts of the UK.

ID: Snake-like body, slate grey with black fins and large eyes, the only other eel they can be confused with is the much smaller silver eel, which is of a yellowish colour and has much smaller eyes.

LESSER-SPOTTED DOGFISH (Scyliorhinus canicula)

This small, very common member of the shark family is hated by some anglers because it grabs baits aimed at larger species. Its presence in large shoals can make fishing for anything else impossible, especially after dark. However, its obliging nature ensure bites, although the LSD can be frustrating to hook for the novice and match angler alike.
Not so prized for eating nowadays, it has successfully re-colonised its old haunts after being decimated by long lines and

trammel nets in the past, when it was a chip shop favourite.

ID: Small shark shape, pinkish in colour with numerous black/brown spots. The dogfish species have eyelids, and close their eyes and squirm when caught. Please return with care or despatch if for eating.

BULL HUSS (Scyliorhinus stellaris)

The larger of the two dogfish, the bull huss or huss is otherwise a carbon copy of the lesser-spotted version, with a mainly south and westerly distribution. It frequents deeper water and rough ground where it feeds on crustaceans and small fish. Its tendency to squirm and roll into a ball when hooked makes it difficult to land, although it cannot be called a strong fighter. Strong tackle is needed, though, because its abrasive skin will rub through mono line.

ID: Any dogfish weighing more than 3lb is likely to be a huss. It has a blunter head than the LSD, and fewer larger spots.

TOPE (Galeorhinus galeus)

The largest of the shark-like species caught from the UK shore, tope are rarely caught from the shore, but it is still possible to hook them from some of the deep water marks off Devon, Wales, the Isle of Man and Ireland. The tope has teeth, making it easy to tell apart from smoothhound. Best baits are mackerel and frozen large sandeel, the latter easier to cast any distance. Strong fighters, tope require a wire bite trace.

ID: Largest of the shore sharks, slender, with a pointed snout, sharp pointed teeth, large and small dorsal fin, plus anal fin.

"(left) Alan Yates proudly displays a shore-caught smoothhound"

Many smaller non-commercial species have thrived because of fewer predators, the resulting increase in the food supply and the fact that they can reproduce inside a couple of years. These are, in many cases, the most common fish around and the target of the freelance or the competition angler.

While it is possible to specialise with a large bait for a large fish, fishing for the smaller species with strong hooks and gear is an acceptable and successful freelance alternative.

BOTTOM FEEDERS
FLATFISH (Families Pleuronectidae, Soleidae, Scophthalmidae and Bothidae)

PLAICE (Pleuronectus platessa)

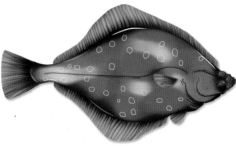

The plaice is the largest of the shore-caught flatfish – only the turbot and halibut are bigger – but they are comparatively rare and taken most often from a boat. The plaice is a sought-after commercial species, and as such its numbers and average size have fallen in many regions over recent decades. It is a relatively slow-growing species. Commonly found in or near estuaries, over clean sand grit bottoms and on sand banks or patches between pea mussel beds inshore, it survives on a diet of marine worms and small crustaceans. It is an inquisitive flatfish and is commonly fished for with bright glitter spoons with sequins and beads. Sometimes floating beads are added to the hook snood and rig for extra appeal.

ID: Distinct bright red/vermillion spots rather than the red or orange flecks of the dab. Smooth skin, right eyed, knobbly top to the head.

SOLE (Solea solea)

The largest of the soles found around the UK, the Dover sole reaches around 4lb, but a 2lb fish is a specimen. It can be found very close to shore, especially after dark. In some regions it is considered nocturnal. Only found on some venues, mostly shell, grit or mud bottoms, but is common on one venue and rare on another a mile away. Small mouth, so an essential when catching soles is hooks of size 2 or below.

ID: The sole shape is distinct, with a hooked mouth.

DAB (Limand limanda)

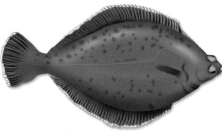

A small flatfish which is common around the UK from sandy, shell grit shorelines. Very popular for eating, it's a prized catch of the freelance angler fishing for the pot. Dabs have a liking for stale lugworms because they hang around and feed on sand bars, where they take advantage of shellfish and worms killed or buried by a storm. Several days after a storm, when the wave action uncovers the dead marine worms, the dabs will be there!

ID: Generally under 1lb, a brown rough-skinned flatfish with a convex tail and pronounced curve in the lateral line.

FLOUNDER (Platichthys flesus)

Once the most common of British fishes, found everywhere, in recent years its common use as pot bait by the commercial crab and whelk fishermen has seen a drastic decline in numbers. It favours brackish water and is commonly found in estuaries and harbours. It swims close to the shore, inside the breakers, and can easily be over-cast.

ID: Rows of bony tubercles at the edge of fins, square-cut tail, scaly head.

TURBOT and BRILL: (Scophthalmus maximus) and (Scophthalmus rhombus)

These species are seldom caught from the shore, although small specimens are taken from Irish strands and North of England beaches on occasions. Both are fish eaters, with a large mouth that can easily engulf a substantial fish bait.

ID: The brill, unlike the turbot, has a frilly edge to the front of the dorsal fin.

"Many anglers choose to fish for pouting, whiting, dabs and dogfish in the hope that they will catch plenty of small fish for the pot, and that a bigger specimen may happen along"

"Plaice – their pronounced vermillion spots set them apart from the other flatfishes"

"*Grey mullet can be caught in marinas, from sheltered backwaters and around piers during summer and autumn*"

OTHER BOTTOM FEEDERS

WHITING (Merlangius merlangius)

A small member of the cod family found in large shoals inshore, especially after dark, whiting can be suicidal in a tide but frustrating to hook in slack water. The average size is less than 1lb, but specimens to 3lb are occasionally caught from the shore. It has a liking for worms and large slices of fresh fish. Small ones make good bait for bass and cod.

ID: Slender, silvery, big eyes, delicate but tiny sharp teeth.

HADDOCK (Melonogrammus aeglefinus)

One of the rarest members of the cod family, the haddock is a deep water species with a northern distribution around the UK, not often seen from the shore nowadays. Similar to the whiting and cod, and from the same family, it is delicate and difficult to return alive.

ID: Black thumb print mark on flanks.

POUTING (Trisopterus luscus)

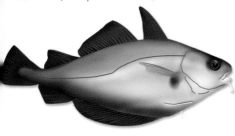

A species more common in the southern UK, it is considered to be a pest except among match anglers. It rapidly loses its bright coloration once dead and is not considered good eating because of its many small bones. It makes a deadly bait on the hook, alive or dead, for bass.

ID: Chin barbel, scales fall off, copper/bronze bars when fresh.

BLACK BREAM
(Spondyliosoma cantharus)

There are several species of bream, the most common being the black bream, which grows to around 4lb but is more commonly caught at under 2lb. A shoal fish that becomes localised around rocks, reefs and weed banks in summer, it has a small mouth, making bites difficult to hook at times.

ID: Silver scaled with large single dorsal fin, small mouth and lips. There is a blue black rim to the tail.

TUB GURNARD (Trigla lucerna)

There are three main species of gurnard, the tub gurnard being the largest of this group of bottom-dwelling fishes. Bright red with blue fins, this bony-headed summer visitor is occasionally caught from the shore on lures and bait.

ID: Large bony head, bright red with large peacock blue fins

SILVER EEL (Anguilla anguilla)

The smaller of the UK eels, also found in freshwater, they travel huge distances to the Sargasso Sea to spawn. At sea they reach a maximum of around 4lb, but much bigger landlocked specimens have been recorded in freshwater. They are considered a pest by many anglers because the small specimens twist and slime-up rigs in their efforts to escape.

ID: Smaller eel, yellow, small eye.

MIDWATER FEEDERS

GREY MULLET (Chelon labrosus)

There are several UK species of mullet, in fact these are among the most common fish worldwide. The thick-lipped grey is the largest UK mullet and the one most anglers concentrate on. It has a reputation for being hard to catch, and locating the 'grey ghost' and getting it to feed are essential tactics. The mullet has a unique digestive system and can survive in unsavoury areas of the estuary on a low quality diet. It scavenges and is often caught on bread and other human throwaways, and even material around sewer outfalls. The smaller thin-lipped mullet is nicknamed the 'kamikaze' mullet for its suicidal tendencies towards hookbaits. Mullet are strong, dogged fighters with unmatched stamina, which is why they have such a cult following.

ID: Thick rubbery lips, striped scale pattern, slimmer torpedo shape than the bass.

MACKEREL (Scomber scombrus)

Mainly considered as bait, the mackerel is an extremely powerful fighter – shame it doesn't grow to 20lb. On light gear, it's a fun fish to catch. Unfortunately it is also reckless when feeding, charging into a shoal of whitebait without any fear. This means anglers can catch the species easily on lures, leading to the reputation of mackerel as being easy prey – only juniors and novices brag about how many mackerel they have caught, and among serious sea anglers catching mackerel other than for bait or the barbecue carries a certain stigma!

ID: Brightly striped blue green fish with large eyes.

Scad: Trachurus trachurus

The scad has a mainly southern distribution and is one of the last of the summer species to arrive, large shoals found around some piers. Has colonised the length of the English Channel in recent years and pushed north. Not closely related to the mackerel, but of similar behaviour, small, good fighter, fun to catch on booms or a float alongside the pier wall, not considered good to eat because of the large number of bones, but small specimens are another excellent bait fished live for big bass.

ID: Bony protrusions at tail, very large eyes and mouth

Garfish: Belone belone

A relative of the marlin with a long beak giving its nickname "Mr Beaky" this unusual eel like species feeds near the surface and is often spotted jumping over seaweed and flotsam. The gar rarely grows bigger than 1lb which is a shame because its acrobatic fight on light tackle is to be seen to be believed. Its internal skeleton is turquoise luminous green giving its other nickname "green bones"

ID: Slender eel like fish with long beaked mouth, turquoise green bones.

Wrasse: Labrus bergylta

Several species of wrasse are common around the UK, but only the Ballan is considered big enough to deliberately target. Nicknamed the rock ruffian it is commonly found around rough ground and weed which it retreats into when hooked. It can be difficult to extract the bigger specimens from their rock cliff home and the fish of record proportions are usually found in the remotest rock marks, some very dangerous to fish. The smaller cuckoo wrasse is very colourful, but rarely beats 1lb.

ID: Flat teeth and rubbery lips designed for removing shell fish from the rocks, scales and green or brown, adults can be red with white spots etc.

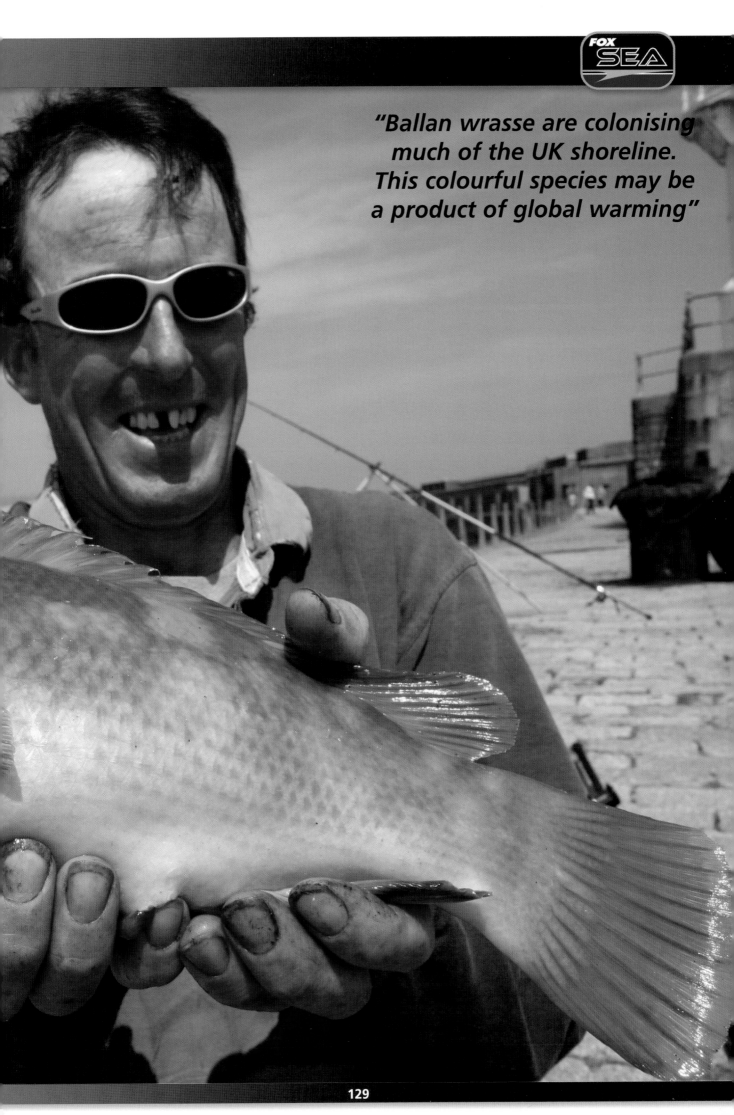

"Ballan wrasse are colonising much of the UK shoreline. This colourful species may be a product of global warming"

Many species of sea fish have spines or teeth, and the general rule is to handle with care, especially anything you are unsure of. Considered the most dangerous are the weever species. Echiichthys vipera, the lesser weever, is common from many summer beaches and is easily confused with a small pouting, bass or whiting. It has a venomous spine on its dorsal fin and on its gill covers and these can penetrate a cloth, so take care. The result of a sting is a painful swelling, best treated with very hot water – in extreme cases, medical treatment is necessary.

The sting ray has a spine on its tail which can inflict a painful wound which has been known to be fatal, although rarely. The venom includes an anti-coagulant which prevents blood clotting, therefore any toxin can reach the blood easily. If stung, seek medical advice.

Most of the small shore sharks like the dogfish have rough, sandpaper-like skin and should be handled with care. Grip the dogfish by it head and tail when removing the hook to prevent it rubbing the skin off your arm.

Bass have spikes and spines and should be handled carefully. As with most of the spiky fishes, holding the small specimens by the mouth is the simplest way to handle them for hook removal.

The spurdog has a sharp bony spine on the leading edges of its dorsal fins, and should be handled with care.

Several of the smaller species have small spikes, spines and sharp teeth. Flatfish have a rib bone that often protrudes above their stomach and can catch an unwary finger. Dragonets have small spines, as do wrasse, scad and bullheads.

"Hold dogfish by the head and tail to prevent their sandpaper-like hide taking your own skin off!"

"Take extra care when unhooking dangerous species like the sting ray"

FISH WELFARE

Some species of fish are tough and can withstand being caught, unhooked and returned. The dogfish, for instance, is a survivor and the ideal species for catch and release. Most of the smaller members of the cod family, on the other hand, are fairly delicate and easily damaged or killed if handled too much or for too long.

Watch an experienced sea angler remove a hook from a fish and it's all over in a blur, but for many novices and even some experienced anglers it can be a traumatic and difficult task, especially if the fish is hooked deeply.

The welfare of the fish is a considerable problem, especially for the novice sea angler, because most sea fish are small, less than 1lb, and the hooks we use as standard – from size 2 to 2/0 – are capable of inflicting major damage to a small fish's mouth unless they are removed extremely carefully.

Preventing fish taking hooks down deeply is not an option. You can use bigger hooks, although when these hook a small fish they may do more damage.

The problem is compounded by the fact that most of the species we catch eat first, swallow second – there is no thinking involved.

Striking early can help, but it is not a consistent solution. Often, the range we fish at and the tackle we use only shows a bite when a fish is already hooked.

Far more effective is to tackle the problem of removing the hook efficiently.

De-hooking quickly and effectively is mostly about angles – you simply need to manoeuvre the hook so that you are pulling against the barb only. Anglers have major problems mainly because they pull against the hook bend. Only practice will make you efficient with the process, and it's a good idea, if you struggle, to get an experienced angler to show you the methods. Once learned, never forgotten.

"Catch and release species like mullet deserve careful handling"

"The Gemini disgorger makes hook removal simple, and saves fingers from damage from the teeth of many of the small species"

Lots of sea anglers use their finger as a disgorger – simply push the forefinger into the bend of the hook, push the hook and remove. It's great for toothless fish, but with others you're asking for minced fingers, so a disgorger is a worthwhile tool to carry at all times.

On of the best disgorgers for use with shore fish is the T-bar used by charter skippers – a mini eyed version for the shore works perfectly on dogfish and whiting. A freshwater disgorger is perfect for removing smaller hooks from flatfish and eels.

TOP TIPS

• If a fish is hooked deeply it is an option to cut the line and leave a hook in situ. Personally I am not a fan of this idea, but if all else fails it may seem there is no other solution. Your conscience is more important than political correctness. Some may be concerned about killing a fish and then throwing it back into the sea dead, others think this more humane than to let it die slowly. My answer is always to eat the fish if it is sizeable, although nothing is wasted if you don't because if a fish does not survive it feeds the birds or the crabs. Remember to sometimes add your hook to a returned tiddler, because big fish eat them too!

• Strictly speaking you can only retain fish that are at or above the legal minimum size limit. However, not all species of commonly-caught sea fish have a legal minimum size. Indeed, the likes of pout, rockling and many others have no size limit at all and can be retained "for the cat".

Minimum fish sizes are set by DEFRA and local fisheries committees, mostly for plate size and not conservation. Minimums can vary. A safe way to avoid a fine is to abide by the minimum sizes set by the angling organisations like the National Federation of Sea Anglers. These are set slightly above the average legal minimums, for obvious reasons.

SOME MINIMUM FISH SIZE LIMITS
Bass – 41 cm
Bream – 25cm
Cod – 35cm
Dab – 23cm
Dogfish – 41cm
Flounder – 25cm
Garfish – 38cm
Mackerel – 30cm
Mullet – 33cm
Plaice – 28cm
Pout – 20cm
Rays – 41cm (measure across wings)
Sole – 25cm
Scad – 25cm
Whiting – 27cm
Wrasse – 23cm
Unclassified – 18cm

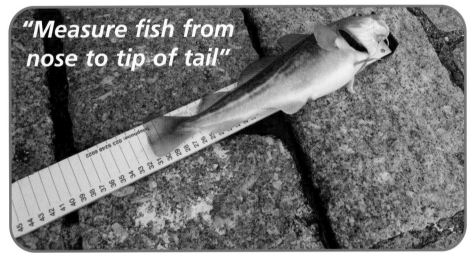
"Measure fish from nose to tip of tail"

TOP TIPS

BAIT

- A flask of hot coffee is great on a cold beach, but in summer you can use a flask to keep your frozen sandeel in top condition. By removing one every cast and tying it on the hook with bait cotton ensures that they stay in top condition and they don't go soft or the bellies burst because they have thawed out.

- A free lined ragworm can be deadly for species like pollack, bass, scad etc in summer. Use a small strong short shank hook (size 1 to 2/0 Kamasan B940S) and just nick the ragworm through the head so that it swims naturally - allow bites to develop and change the worm if its tail is bitten off.

- Lots of sea anglers only want to buy large ragworm and lugworm because they offer better value for money, but depending upon what you are fishing for the size of the worm can make a difference to results. Small worms are more effective for catching small fish, large worms are best for specimen fish. Ask your tackle dealer for the size worms you need, or request a mix of sizes for general fishing.

- Can't face handling ragworm because of their nippy pincers? Cut the head off with your scissors before baiting!

- One of the best all-round summer hook baits is peeler crab tipped with a fresh sliver of mackerel. It's deadly for a range of species from smoothhound to ray, especially off the beach after dark. It's good for dogfish too.

WEATHER

- Trouble with rain on your glasses when fishing? Get one of the latest long curved peaked baseball-type hat. You will be surprised at the difference it makes.

- Whilst beach fishing shelters and giant umbrellas are all the rage, but they are often not as practical as a smaller fishing umbrella. Check out the Argos catalogue company for a cheap 45 inch umbrella. They last as long as those sold for 3 times the price and are far more stable in strong winds.

DIY

- Replacing the rubber floor mats in your car? Don't throw the old ones away. When cut up they make great none-slip rod rests for fishing from walled piers to prevent your rod sliding along the wall and getting scratched or damaged.

- Don't you just hate the way that the bottom of a tackle rucksack sags out of shape and lets in water? However, solve the problem with a plastic washing-up bowl or plastic cat litter tray?

- You can whip a Starlite on your rod tip quickly and easily with elastic bait cotton. Run the cotton around the Starlite 30 times and then around the length of the Starlite to lock the cotton in the joint between it and the rod tip.

- Loose spigot joint? Are two sections touching each other? Then you need to see your rod builder. A DIY solution is to build up the male spigot with a carbon spray or a quick and easy, but temporary on the beach solution, is to build up the male spigot with candle wax.

- You can save wear and tear on your waders and chest waders by hanging them up when they are not in use. Left wet and crumpled in a corner you are inviting punctures.

- A pack of waterproof plasters are a must in the tackle box or rucksack for those little accidents. However, even the best plasters come lose when wet, so a roll of surgical tape is the perfect solution to keeping a finger plaster in place.

CHAPTER 5
THE BAITS

It is common knowledge among regular sea anglers that using the correct bait for a particular species from a particular venue at a particular time of year is very important - Is it not? I tell you what, three quarters of sea anglers neglect facts that stare them in the face regarding the best baits and catch less because of it.

The diversity of the hook baits used around the UK coast relates to the species sought, the type of seabed and the availability of baits. Where baits are common and easy to obtain they tend to be popular and used by a majority. This throws up many anomalies in angler's preference for baits and suggests that some are better than others.

Lugworm for example, ask any angler what is the best bait for sea angling and lugworm will invariably be the answer. But lugworm is easily obtained in commercial quantities by diggers and dealers and is used by the majority and this is a major reason why it catches the most fish, not because it's always the best bait. So before you generalise or dismiss any bait, be certain that you have got the facts right because around the coast in many regions baits that are less popular can sometimes be very effective at certain times of year, far more deadly than lugworm.

It is surprising how many anglers will spend hundreds of pounds on a rod and reel and then skimp on bait. But the bait on your hook is the link you have to the fish that you can influence. Fish are habitual as well as opportunist feeders and they have an instinct for a free meal. When for instance a gale rips through a sand bar or rock reef they will be on fin to mop up the casualties and in many cases they have tunnel vision for the marine food item that is most available, just as they do in seasons when a particular marine food is plentiful. Using a particular baits when the fish are looking for something else and ignoring the alternatives is the most common reason why sea anglers do not catch fish!

"Big baits for big fish, don't skimp on your bait"

WHITE RAGWORM

White ragworm is widely accepted as a specialist matchfishing bait, and is one of the most effective for catching tiddlers. Considered an essential scratching bait by match anglers, the smaller white ragworm are most effective when tipped on a lugworm to add movement. The larger pearl-coloured white ragworm, also called 'snakes', are a prized winter match bait, effective for codling, dogfish and some other species.

In many regions the white ragworm is considered most effective in the New Year, and this has a lot to do with the worm being gouged from the sand by the winter gales. It's a superb hookbait for some of the midwater species in summer when

head-hooked and fished from piers on booms or under a float and allowed to swim on the hook. It's not readily available from dealers, so you will need to dig your own or find a digger who will supply you.

ROCK WORM

Not as common as the other ragworm, these worms, as their name suggests, are found in rock – mainly chalk and clay – and usually only in regions with white cliffs. They are dug with a small hand pick or heavy fork, and are one of the toughest and wriggliest members of the ragworm family. They are highly favoured as a midwater bait in clear seas, although because of limited availability their use and even the knowledge that they exist is localised. They are among the few ragworm which, after being threaded on the hook and cast out for 20 minutes, stay alive to pinch you on the retrieve! Not available from dealers.

"White ragworm and peeler crab – the two most effective shore baits when the going gets tough"

PEELER CRABS

Peeler crab is an exceptional rough and mixed ground bait which stays on the hook longer than worms, which the crabs remove quickly. In certain situations crab will be left alone by other crabs. One of the most versatile baits available to the sea angler, it catches most shore species and is a highly scented and juicy bait, capable of attracting fish from a distance.

All crustaceans have to shed their shell to grow bigger, and in the case of the crabs this is the only time they can mate.
In early spring and through summer the rising water temperature prompts the cock crabs to peel in large numbers.
This mass moult turns into a race for the cock crab to find a mate. He then protects the hen crab while she peels, and when she is soft the crabs mate. Find two crabs, one on top of the other, and the bottom one will be a hen. If she is belly to belly with the cock crab she will be soft – if not belly to belly she will be a peeler.
Most anglers consider the cock peeler crabs to be the best hookbait. These are larger and juicier, but are found alone.

Once they have peeled their shell, crabs are jelly-like and helpless for a short space of time before the shell hardens.
Fish know this, and move inshore to feast when the crabs are peeling. As hookbaits, crabs are best when they are just about to shed their shell. Once peeled, they are only any good as a large bait used whole for big fish like bass and cod. This is because they quickly harden and are then known as 'crinklies' or 'crispies'.

Peeler crab is a classic example of why fish sometimes have tunnel vision towards a food item – fish seeking soft and shedding crabs in season will totally ignore all other baits.

Use a quarter crab to tip a worm bait, a half for the small species, or a whole one for the large. Varieties include the common shore crab, the edible and the velvet swimmer (the latter two species are subject to a legal minimum size limit).
In recent years spider crabs have increased in numbers around UK shores.
Although these are not so prized as common shore peelers, in some regions spiders can still be effective.

A common problem for anglers is that they try to use crabs that are not yet ready to peel, and these lack the deadly juices of the crabs just about to pop out of their shells. Frozen crabs, too, can be poor if they are frozen after they die.

Peeler crabs are plentiful in spring and early summer in some regions and can be obtained from dealers – in winter a supply is available from South West rivers touched by the warm Gulf Stream, which prompts crabs to peel virtually all year.

HERMIT CRABS

Hermit crabs live in a whelk shell and are an excellent substitute for peeler crab, especially as a bait for smoothhound and ray. Their soft abdomen is also an excellent bait for bream. You can collect hermits with a small baited drop net or pot. The are not easy to keep alive without an air pump, and most boat skippers keep them in a sack hung over the side at their mooring.
Often the hermit will have a small ragworm in the rear of its shell which shares its meals.

LIVE PRAWNS AND SANDEEL

Float fished live prawns are recognised as a specialist bait for bass, pollack and pout during the summer and autumn months. They are float fished alive alongside piers and rocks. It's important to mount the prawn on a hook without killing it, and this is usually done by pushing the hook through a segment near the tail.
Prawns need to be collected with a hand or drop net, and can only be kept alive with an air pump and airstone.

Live sandeel fished on a long trace or freelined are deadly for bass and pollack, and a number of other species.
Again, it is essential not to hook them fatally and so they are hooked through the lips. Use a Fox BH bass hook size 3/0 to 4/0 which is lightweight and ideal for livebaits. Add a Fox bait flag to the point of the hook to lock on your livebait.

SHELLFISH

All shellfish are best when they are local to a shoreline, especially after a gale has dislodged them from their habitat and scattered or buried them, dying, inshore. The fish are used to finding them in a decayed state, unearthed days later, and that's why slightly 'off' shellfish are often more effective than fresh. The likes of razorfish, mussels, clams and butterfish make an excellent bait for lots of species, and it's always worth taking a walk along the shoreline where you are fishing after a gale – sometimes you can pick up a bucketful, and that's when they fish best. Beware of forgotten shellfish, though, the smell is something else!

CLAMS

There are several different clams, but by far the most effective for bait is the piddock clam. This is found in colonies, burrowing in clay/chalk rock, the same habitat as the rock worm. Dig them with a fork or a small pick.

They freeze down well and catch local to the region they are found in. One big advantage with this bait is that they can be returned to the freezer after use and improve with age.

COCKLES, LIMPETS AND MUSSELS

The largest queen cockle has a bright pink 'foot' which is an excellent bait for codling and dabs in regions where they are washed inshore after a winter gale.

Slipper limpets are not native to the UK, but they have colonised many coastal areas, and when a gale dashes them on the shore the fish move in to feast. They are excellent for bass, flounder and other surf species.

Mussels are a popular cocktail rock bait and an alternative for peeler crab in some areas, specially the north of England and Scotland. They are a good standby, and are readily available all year round from the fishmonger.

FISH BAITS

Lots of species of fish switch to a fish diet when they grow large because worms, crabs and the like can no longer sustain their demand for food. It's no coincidence that fish baits hold most of the national records. It's the oily fish that make the best baits, and these include mackerel, herring and sprat.
Any small fish is food for the larger predators, with small pout, smelt, pollack, whiting, sandeels and whitebait among those that can be used as bait.

MACKEREL

By far the most productive fish bait there is because it is highly scented, oily and bloody, it catches most species, especially when fresh. The head and guts, or the popular flapper, are great for big fish like conger, and a small sliver the ideal worm tip-off for whiting. A thin sliver of mackerel belly is great float fished for garfish and mackerel themselves.
Fresh is best, because once mackerel die the texture of their flesh softens and the bait is not so attractive to the fish.

HERRING AND SPRAT

Underrated from the shore, these fish are best when they are in season locally. The only drawback is, these are soft-fleshed fish and, like most fish baits, they lose their effectiveness when several days old. Fresh is best, with fillets, slices, slivers and cutlets all used as baits.
Beware – large, unsupported fish baits are prone to fold up when cast or as they sink and mask the hookpoint. Herring is particularly good for thornback ray, and sprat for big dabs in the New Year.

LIVEBAITS

Because a livebait can be bulky, and long casting will kill it, is not practical to fish from the shore at long range with a live fish. The solution is a livebait rig.
This involves a small size 2 hook which is baited and tied to the shank of a larger 6/0 hook. The rig is cast, and hopefully a small fish will take the small baited hook and in turn be eaten, complete with the big hook, by a cod. Surprisingly effective, this method is the ideal winter ploy for a second rod.

A big hook with a small baited hook can be cast long distances, you then wait for a small fish to take the bait and a cod to take the small fish.

Small live pouting, whiting, pollack and smelt can all be used as livebaits for species like bass. The most common method, when long casting is not required, is to simply lip-hook the live fish and present it on a long trace, either fixed or running, so that it can swim free (below). This method is very effective after dark at close range for bass.

The best livebaits in order are: pouting, whiting, smelt, sandeel, pollack and various other small fish.

"The live bait rig can be a fixed paternoster (shown) or a running trace. Essentials include a strong 6/0 hook and minimum 30lb line. Remember to set your reel drag because takes can be violent at short range"

"Mackerel baits caught a majority of the UK and Irish record fish"

Small fish are the major prey of cod and bass.

A mackerel head or flapper is the ultimate bait for big fish.

A fillet or slice of mackerel in various sizes can be used to target different species.

One mackerel produces a variety of hook baits.

Most baits used by sea anglers can be frozen, and the process actually improves the attractiveness of some of them, while in others the change to the texture that freezing brings ruins them completely. A good example is lugworm which, when frozen, become soft, pappy and next to useless – only black lugworm lends itself to being frozen. Meanwhile, sandeel actually improves as a bait with freezing. This could be due to the change in the texture, allowing the blood and juices to escape the bait more rapidly. Whatever the reason, frozen sandeel catches far more than a fresh dead sandeel, and the only thing better than both is a live one on the hook.

It is imperative that only fresh bait is frozen, and a golden rule when using frozen baits is never to put them back in the freezer once thawed! In fact, a good idea is to treat your frozen baits as if they were YOUR food, and that includes freezer ratings and use by dates.

Beware of freezing lots of one bait in a block. It is essential to freeze it in small batches so that you can remove only what you need from the freezer.
Also consider a rotation system of baits, so that you don't keep any for longer than a season.

Freeze baits as quickly as you can – peeler crab, for instance, deteriorates rapidly once peeled and it's essential to freeze it within an hour of peeling. One method of doing this with a domestic freezer is to have a steel tray already in there, chilled, and then lay the peeled crabs on it before wrapping in clingfilm.

Commercial frozen baits are often vacuum packed and this brings advantages because it excludes air, which can cause freezer burns. Place your baits inside a sealable sandwich-type bag and then push them down into a bucket of water. This will expel all the air, and free up more freezer space.

SQUID
Squid is generally obtained frozen – only occasionally will you find the larger English squid fresh at a fish market. Fished whole, a small Calamari squid is one of the best big-fish baits around, while multi-squid baits are a favourite big bait for keeping unwanted species like dogfish as well as hungry crabs off the hook. Squid fishes best when fresh – beware of stale squid that has travelled in and out of the freezer. When it is off it turns pink!

Most tackle shops sell frozen squid in small packs of two to four. A more economical way to buy squid is from the supermarket in 1lb to 7lb catering boxes. Thaw slightly and split the squid into manageable numbers, bag and re-freeze.

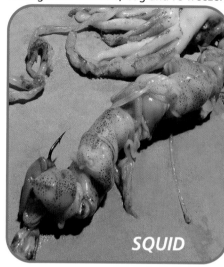

SQUID

FROZEN PEELER CRABS
Be wary of buying these from a tackle dealer. Often, unsold dead or dying crabs are frozen down for the winter, and until they thaw out this fact is difficult to determine. Crabs that have been frozen dead are of no use as bait – their black flesh and gills are a sure sign they have been treated like this.

Freezing surplus peeler crabs during the spring to use as bait the following winter is worth considering to provide a constant supply. It is essential that the crabs are close to shedding their shells and ready to use on the hook. Hard crabs that are not yet fully ready to peel are next to useless fresh, let alone frozen.

Soft crabs do not freeze so well. Peel each crab, wash under the tap and freeze them in tinfoil or plastic freezer wrap.

Freeze peeler crabs when fresh – wrap them in cling film or foil.

SANDEEL
Sandeel are a major frozen bait, and the freezing process actually improves their effectiveness. A year-round bait, frozen sandeel is underrated in many regions. Fished whole, or in sections to tip off other baits, it catches both summer and winter species, while trickled just above the kelp on a spinning rod it is deadly for big pollack. It must be kept frozen before use because it deteriorates quickly. You can use a cool bag for this, although more popular is a wide-mouthed vacuum flask.

Ammo is by far the best quality frozen sandeel available. Some of the other frozen sandeel companies offer very low quality eels, while some tackle dealers do not look after their frozen baits, letting them defrost and then re-freezing them.

SANDEEL

FROZEN PRAWNS
There are a variety of frozen shrimps and prawns available from the supermarket fish counter. We are not talking here about cooked prawns, but fresh frozen examples. A relatively new bait on the sea scene, imported farmed prawns and the likes of tiger prawns are an excellent winter filler when marine worms are in short supply. They can be obtained from most of the supermarket chains which have a fish counter – try Sainsburys, Asda and Morrisons.

You can bait them whole or in small sections tipped on the point of the hook after a lugworm. The latter is an excellent cocktail for general shore and boat angling. Used whole, the prawns need to be tied on to the hook with elastic cotton.

First, remove the shell from the prawn and then thread the hook – a 1/0 Arma Point MA Aberdeen is the perfect size – through the tail end of the prawn so that the hook point protrudes from the thick end of the bait. Wrap several turns of elastic cotton around the prawn and the bend of the hook to lock it in position.

"Peeler crabs for freezing need to be fresh and about to shed their shell. A wet towel keeps crabs in peak condition prior to freezing"

FROZEN FISH BAITS

There are lots of different frozen fish baits available, including many that dealers have frozen themselves. I will repeat that the best frozen baits are those from firms like Ammo, who blast-freeze baits rapidly to retain all the juices.

Freezing tends to soften the flesh of fish baits, especially if not frozen fresh, so it's a good idea to catch and freeze the likes of mackerel as quickly as you can.

The following is a list of the most popular frozen sea baits, with a few easy to follow rules to remember, plus a few artificial alternatives.

BLUEYS

A trade name for an imported species which has flesh like a herring. However, the fillets are less flaky which makes them more suitable for the hook. This is a very oily bait.

ALTERNATIVE BAITS AND ARTIFICIALS

Most times, nothing beats real fresh bait – the likes of lugworm, crab, sandeel and squid will catch most species of UK sea fish. However, when the standard baits are in short supply anglers have to turn to the alternatives. Although most will never match the results of fresh baits, they do occasionally catch fish.

EARTHWORMS

In some river estuaries, earthworms catch flounders and eels at times when flood water is draining into them. Earthworms tend to bleach white in salt water, however, and are less effective than lug or ragworm.

BREAD

Bread is not a natural marine bait, but it does find its way into the sea via the local café, boats and people feeding birds, and it catches a number of sea species, notably mullet. Used in a bread bag hung from the pier wall or in a shirvy mixed with fish and scattered on the rocks as the tide rises, it has been responsible for luring bream, garfish, pout, pollack and bass.

ARTIFICIAL WORMS GULP/JELLY WORMS

Many of these realistic-looking worms, crabs, prawns and so on give poor results when fished static on the sea bed and in very coloured water conditions. They rely in the main for their success on movement and clear water. As with most baits, results improve as competition for food increases and so around a busy wreck, with lots of fish chasing after little food, lesser 'baits' may be taken by hungry fish on an 'eat first, taste later' basis! From the shore, food is shared between fewer fish and so they can take longer to be selective and examine baits closely.

BAIT ADDITIVES

Bait additives are commonly used, and are said to be successful in freshwater fishing, but at sea they are not nearly so deadly. This has a lot to do with strong currents washing them away quickly and fish having that tunnel vision to the target food – they know what they are looking for, and additives won't sway them.

Beware of bait additives which catch more anglers than fish. At times we are all suckers for a sales story, but most of the magic additives and flavours don't stay in favour long when anglers discover they don't work. Several have come and gone, and will doubtless appear containing the amino acids that induce fish to feed – but as yet there is nothing to beat real, fresh, quality baits like peeler crab and yellowtail lugworm.

Some anglers use WD40 as a bait spray additive and reckon it works, but then there will always be those who want to put a good result down to a single 'magic' bait additive when the fact is, success is attributable to a combination of elements.

COCKTAIL BAITS

Mixing several baits is a popular tactic to enhance the hook offering, and such baits are called 'cocktails'. There are no hard and fast rules – you can combine all types of baits. Some, like peeler crab and lugworm, are highly scented; some, like small ragworm, offer movement with their wriggly tails; while squid and fish reflect light and appear white in clear water. Certain baits attract particular species, and so the angler can use a variety of combinations to improve on a single hookbait and make it more attractive to species being targeted.

Lugworm is the basis of many of the popular cocktail baits (lugworm tipped with anything). Squid, clam, fish, crab, ragworm – the combinations are endless, the lugworm being enhanced by scent, colour and/or movement. The rules are simple – anything goes – and this includes cocktails of more than two baits. Adding anything to lugworm can make it more versatile for all species and seasons.

The most common pitfall when using a cocktail bait is to put too much bait on a small hook. This can slip and bunch around the bend, masking the point.

FAVOURITE COCKTAILS

Peeler crab tipped with a small sliver of fresh mackerel is a very effective cocktail for lots of summer species.

Lugworm tipped with a fingernail-sized sliver of squid is the ideal all-round cocktail. It catches cod, whiting, dab, pout, dogfish, bream and lots more.

Lugworm tipped with a small white ragworm is a favourite match fishing bait for a host of the small species.

Lugworm tipped with half a peeler crab is a great cocktail for codling, cod, flounder, pout and coalfish.

Lugworm tipped with a small sliver of fish or squid is perhaps the best winter bait combination, especially for whiting. A fish tip also catches flounders in many northern regions; in the south it is better to tip with one of the ragworm species.

White ragworm tipped with a sliver of mackerel or sandeel is a deadly match fishing cocktail for dogfish.

BAIT TIPS

- While peeler crab is a deadly bait for codling, it is less effective for the bigger cod. Lugworm, or a lugworm and squid cocktail, or even a live fish, are at the top of the cod's bait list.

- Run out of mackerel lures? Cut the gill edges off the mackerel you have caught and put them on your hook – they make deadly mackerel attractors.

- The tougher yellowtail or black lugworm stay on the hook longer than the thin skinned common lugworm, and although they cost more, you do not need so many for a session.

- Peeled crab legs and claws baited on their own or as part of a cockail are worth a try, and will catch anything from pouting to bass.

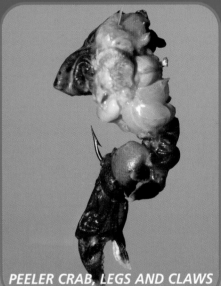

PEELER CRAB, LEGS AND CLAWS

- Don't limit your cocktails to just two baits. Peeler crab, mussel and lugworm all make a great cocktail for winter rock fishing for cod.

MIXED COCKTAILS

"Lugworm tipped with white ragworm is the most deadly for the smaller species. Lug-tipped squid catches lunkers"

Watch any experienced sea angler bait his hook and it all appears so easy – but where does the novice start, what are the techniques for baiting a hook, and how do you ensure that a bait stays on the hook in a position that will not mask the point?

It is not always essential to present your bait to the fish as a faithful example of the living item, and it is unnecessary to cover or hide the hook completely. Sea fish are used to finding their food dead and damaged and they are certainly not aware of hooks because in the main they are killed when caught. With the growth in popularity of catch and release, maybe sea fish will become more hook and line aware, like their freshwater cousins. This has already happened in some regions with mullet, but generally you can bait up with the main emphasis on hooking the fish, rather than hiding the hook!

The first step is to match the hook to the bait type and size – especially the size. It's literally pointless to bury a size 2 hook in a whole squid. You need a 6/0. Likewise, a single lugworm threaded on a 6/0 would look lost. You need a size 2.

The modern approach to shore angling is to lean towards small baits for the smaller species at times when big fish are scarce. This tactic involves the use of very strong, but small, hooks. Freshwater carp anglers have shown us that very big fish can be landed on such hooks, although a size 4 would seem to be the smallest size the sea angler would need to go down to. Certainly a strong size 2 is the minimum for most situations. Fishing with smaller, lighter hooks than a size 4 is still alien to most UK anglers, so let's not get carried away by the Continental fishing style when we don't have to be!

THE TOOLS

To aid your bait presentation you will need a few tools. Scissors are essential for cutting fish and crabs, or for trimming a finished bait. A knife is essential to cut slivers and strips, and most anglers choose a quality filleting knife because this will also help prepare the catch for eating.

Bait elastic is an essential. It helps you secure the bait for casting and keeps it on the correct part of the hook – what you do not want is the bait slipping down the shank and ending up in the bend, where it masks the hookpoint!

A baiting needle is a great help to the novice sea angler for baiting worms. Simply thread the worm on the needle, put the hookpoint in the hole in the end of the needle and, with the hook snood tight, slide the worm from needle to hook. Two different types of needle are available. For lugworm a thicker, blunt needle is essential because it is easier to thread through the middle of the worm. For ragworm you need a thinner, sharper needle that can puncture the head of the worm and then thread through the body of the bait.

Here are two baits that require a little time and attention to detail to mount on the hook efficiently – careful presentation will ensure that the hook works efficiently and hooks the fish! How many anglers bait up their hooks so that they look perfect on the pier or beach, then thrash the guts out of the bait on the cast so that it ends up in a ball on the seabed? A fish grabs the bait, miles away from the hookpoint, pulls the bait from the hook and swims away with a free meal.

BAITING LUGWORM

Okay, so baiting a lugworm on a hook is no big deal. A long shank hook makes the worm easier to thread, and in general all the angler then needs to do is pass the hookpoint through the worm.
Cast it out and gravity presents the bait around the hookpoint. However, there are little tricks that at times help with lugworm. One, when using black lug that are a little too big or soft, is to wrap the worm around the hook several times as you 'sew' the point through the first inch. This locks the bait in position around the hook eye and stops it sagging too far down the shank or around the point.

Which end of a lugworm goes on the hook first? Most anglers break off the sandy tail and thread the worm tail-first, reasoning that the hookpoint is then in the juiciest head end of the worm, but this is not gospel. You are free to make your own mind up which is the better tactic.

It is, however, very important to ensure that the hook goes through the centre of the worm, and that no loops of worm are left sticking out from the bait for the fish to grab and tear the worm off the hook.

OTHER BAITS

There are other baits that require more attention – more delicate baits that can be destroyed by casting or gravity. Here, a small roll or spool of baiting elastic is an essential aid to good bait presentation. It is important, though, that you use the right grade of elastic! There are several on the market, some of the toughest being ideal for huge multi-squid boat baits. Medium elastic is great for shore fishing, but if you are fussy there are now some really fine Continental bait elastics available too.
The thinking behind the lighter elastic is that it can be removed easily without threatening your sanity when you clear the hook to re-bait, and it does not impede any fish taking the bait.

LUGWORM ON A PENNELL RIG

"Bloody, juicy, scented yellowtail lugworm are the best for most winter species"

"Fish are accustomed to finding their food beaten up by the sea, so take care to mount baits so that the hook can be affective, don't mask the point"

BAITING RAGWORM

Ragworm vanishes from the hook quicker than lugworm, so in most cases it pays to put two worms on the hook rather than just one if you are using ragworm on that hook alone.

Large king ragworm have pincers which can nip unwary fingers, and this does deter a few anglers from using them. The answer is to nip off the head section with your scissors before threading them on the hook. You can also cut the worm into sections to thread on the hook.

WRIGGLING TAILS

For a wriggling bunch of ragworm, thread the first worm completely on the hook, then head-hook all subsequent worms. This ensures the bait stays on when cast and allows both scent and movement to emanate from the bait.

BAITING SQUID

The Pennell rig is essential for baiting a whole squid, because of the length of the bait – if you try to fish it on a single hook it sags around the point. Using a two-hook

Pennell you can pass the lower hook through the top of the squid, wrap the line around it several times and then put the hook in the head. The top sliding hook is then nicked into the top of the squid to support it and lock it in position.

For slivers of squid, pass the hookpoint through the bait, then twist the bait and pass the hook through the same side. This locks the sliver into position near the hookpoint.

BAITING SANDEEL

Leave a packet to thaw and within an hour the bellies will burst, but keep them frozen right up until when you put them on the hook and they will stay in perfect condition and be far easier to thread and secure on the hook.

SANDEEL

Once it's out of the flask, chop off the head and tail of the sandeel. Chop the head off close to the gills. This area is the bloodiest! A 1/0 is the perfect size hook for sandeel, but you can use bigger or smaller to suit the fish you seek. From the tail end, pass the hookpoint through the sandeel for 4cm, then pull the hook completely out. Push the hookpoint back into the eel 5cm further down until it comes out of the end with the gills.

You will now have an eel baited on the shank of the hook with the hook eye and knot exposed in the middle of the eel and the hookpoint protruding just where the

eel is oozing blood and juices.

From the hookpoint end, wrap the eel tightly with elastic cotton. Take special care to wrap several turns either side of the exposed hook eye and knot. This locks the eel in position. Continue for the length of the sandeel.

PEELER CRAB

A whole peeler, average size 4cm, fits a 3/0 to 4/0 hook. First step is to cut the crab almost in half from top to bottom, then open it out lengthways and lay it along the hook shank. Whip with cotton, especially around the hook eye. Add a few peeled legs or claws to the hookpoint to complete the bait.

PEELER CRAB ON A PENNELL RIG

For half a crab, use a size 1 to 1/0 hook and thread the point in and out of each leg socket. This will secure it, but for power casting wrap a few turns of elastic around the eye end of the hook for extra security.

Large crab baits used on a two-hook Pennell rig are best secured on the lower hook, with the top sliding hook nicked into the top of the bait – this, in effect, hair-rigs the bait and is an effective tactic for cod and bass.

"Three productive cocktail combinations"

LUG/SHELLFISH

LUG/WHITE RAGWORM

LUG/CRAB

- When baiting with bunches of ragworm, dunk the tails in the sea prior to casting. This binds them together, preventing the cast spraying them off – try it, it really does work!

- For small ragworm, choose hooks with a small eye. These are easier to thread through the worms without breaking them up.

- The number of holes you put in a worm when threading the hook through it makes a difference to the scent escaping into the sea. In situations where there are lots of fish, the quicker the scent releases, the sooner the fish will find it. A baiting needle allows you to put the bait on the hook with fewer puncture holes in it, and that way the scent trail will last longer.

LUG ON A BAITING NEEDLE

- When using a bait additive, pre-bait your hooks and soak them in additive before you go fishing, then freeze and place the baited snoods in a flask.

- Double patting is a popular method used by match anglers to cut the time between casts. However, leaving a ready baited rig hanging on the rod rests mean vital fish-attracting juices will drip from it.

- Small fish baits like sprat are soft and difficult to keep on the hook. Cut into cutlets and pass the hookpoint through the bone in the middle of the bait and it will stay on the hook longer.

- Replacing a washed out bait every cast is essential to ensure a positive and lasting scent trail.

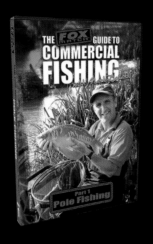

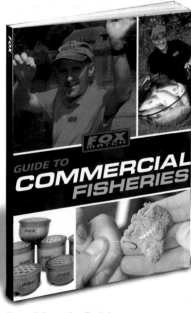

CHAPTER 6
BAIT DIGGING AND WELFARE

Collecting or digging your own bait brings a number of advantages, not least of these being a wide knowledge and awareness of the variety of baits available, their habitats and the fish they catch. On the way to obtaining a supply you learn why and when fish switch to the different baits, all about the tides and – a bonus – you help keep yourself fit into the bargain.

Digging a supply of worms or collecting peeler crabs and shellfish can be a tedious and time-consuming task, but is something the angler can do to enhance his fishing and improve his results. While the basic baits are available from the tackle shop, they are never of the variety of a self-collected supply. Make no mistake, sea angling is a complex sport with local knowledge, experience and effort all major keys to success. The best tackle is useless without good bait, and making an effort to obtain the most effective baits is a short cut to consistent results. All you require are a couple of buckets, boots or waders, and a fork or bait pump.

THE TIDES

It is obvious that you can only dig bait when the tide is out, although because the height varies from tide to tide and from day to day, some tides are better than others for low tide bait collection. The highest spring tides are also the lowest tides, with the sea going out the furthest and often exposing virgin sand. These are best for worm digging. The neap tides are the shortest, and not so good. A standard tide table will show the tide times, plus the height of each low and high tide. From this information you can discover the best tides for digging bait as well as fishing.

Marine worms and other organisms live at different locations over the tide's range. Most tides will allow you to dig the common lugworm and, in many cases, king ragworm. However, black lugworm, white ragworm and fish are just a few of the baits that are usually available only during the lowest tides.

The weather plays its part, because the tide and water levels can be affected by strong winds, sometimes many thousands of miles away. A large swell can make a low-tide venue unreachable, even during the lowest spring tide, while a wind from a certain direction can prevent the sea from reaching its normal low water mark. Occasionally the wind blows the sea further out on a venue.

Knowing the conditions that produce this situation can create a bait digger's bonanza. You can then reach beds that are rarely uncovered.

HOW MUCH BAIT DO I NEED?

The answer to this question is 'plenty'. Always take more bait than you need, but the rule is, don't waste any. It may be a conservation issue with some anglers to skimp on bait, but it is not good angling sense to be on a venue with the fish climbing the rod tip, only to find you have run out of bait!

Most anglers who dig their own bait find they can never get enough worms – the pressure on some regions' bait beds means that potential supplies are far less than in the past, although on others supplies are maintained because worms are pushed inshore by the weather. Whatever your fortunes on a venue, setting up a bait fridge is worthwhile because bait need never then be wasted. It is possible to keep all types of bait alive indefinitely in a fridge, even more so in one with a marine aeration system.

After you fish, any surplus bait can be returned to the bait fridge, and that ensures you will always have a ready bait supply for those opportunist trips when the fish suddenly appear.

Remember, too, that the best spring tides for bait digging only occur every fortnight. Between them are the shortest neap tides, when bait beds cannot be reached and some baits are particularly scarce from the dealers who rely on the professional diggers.

Keeping worms alive that were dug during the spring tides for use during the neap tides confers a big advantage over those who rely on the tackle dealer. Obviously, for the competition angler, this advantage cannot be ignored, while for the non-match angler it's the difference between going fishing and not!

Top Tip - Even if the bait you have over from a session is no longer fresh or alive, it can be taken home and frozen for use as groundbait for future sessions.

Some baits are worth their weight in gold!

"Enough of the correct bait is crucial to success. Don't spend a fortune on tackle and then skimp on bait."

"The larger cock peeler crabs are the juiciest and come from the thickest estuary mud. Tyres, drain pipes, guttering and old tiles can all be used as crab traps"

VENUES

Low tide venues differ, and although there is generally some form of useable hook bait everywhere it is not always present in sufficient quantity to make it worth digging or collecting. Oddly enough, where there is lots of bait, fish are often scarce, and vice-versa. This is because it's the shallow, sheltered regions of the coast where the marine life forms can establish themselves. On the wind-exposed storm coasts, worms and shellfish have a job to keep their foothold. For this reason, the best places to dig and collect bait are estuaries and the sheltered beaches and bays that surround them.

The bigger worms tend to be nearer to the low-tide mark, because that region is not dug so much, but they are not necessarily the best worms – many anglers complain about those who dig in the 'brood' at the top of the beach, although in truth these worms can sometime be the best and easiest to dig, especially in the depths of winter during rain and snow. The important thing is to leave them alone until such times!

Various types of sea bed are preferred by the different baits. Lugworm in general prefer clean sand, although they can sometime be found in a mix of sand, mud and stones. Different grounds can affect their 'taste' to the fish, and that is why worms from some regions are more popular than others – they simply catch more fish. Digging your own worms allows you to decide which of the worms YOU want to use, rather than those that the professionals can dig the most of!

King ragworm and harbour ragworm, or maddies, are generally found in soft or stony black mud in sheltered estuaries and harbours. The latter often prefer the mud close to a freshwater stream, and both have periods of the year when breeding makes them less effective as bait.

In some regions, ragworm feed on green weed in late summer and this tends to make them softer and more difficult to keep alive for any length of time.

The large pearl-coloured white ragworm prefer mixed sand and shale, and a giveaway to their presence are patches of tube worms which protrude from the sand like thin, light-brown straws.

They are always found close to the low tide extremities. The smaller white ragworm (cat worms) are mostly found in clean sand, often among lugworm, nearer the high tide mark and close to the surface. Dig these into a bucket of clean sea water and change the water before you take them home. They keep very well in sea water in the fridge in trays, but as with all the worms, don't crowd too many together – 10 to 15 a tray will be plenty.

Peelers of common shore crabs are found everywhere – harbours, rock reefs, around groynes in soft mud, under rocks or in sea weed in rockpools, in fact in any hiding place they can find, sometimes very close to the high tide mark.

Most of the shellfish live below the low tide extreme and tend to be moved inshore by large seas on the storm beaches. Their foothold on life can be tenuous. Razorfish prefer the lower regions of the tide line and can be found among tube worms and on low-tide sand bars. Butter fish, which are a small clam, are found in many regions where there are razorfish.

Mussels are available in most sheltered coastal regions, where they colonise walls, groyne posts and rocks. The biggest mussels are often found on Atlantic coasts.

"Yellowtail lugworm have a perfectly spherical cast (right). The common lugworm's cast is broken coils (inset)"

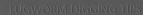

DIGGING YOUR OWN LUGWORM

Finding a venue where there is a good number of quality worms is essential if you want a bucketful – you can be pickier if you want a particular size or type of worm. Common lugworm are comparatively simple to dig in most regions with a fork. Just dig trench-style as you would potatoes. A flat-tined potato fork is best, with its wide tines ideal for lifting the sand from the hole as you dig. The professional diggers actually have the tines/prongs of their forks ground down to suit the type of worm or venue they are digging on, and you will generally find that this is a short cut to obtaining the best digging forks. An old, worn fork will be lighter, with better penetration of the sand, because the tines are thinner and sharper.

Lugworm live in a U-shaped burrow. The depth of the U and where the worm is in the burrow varies between common and yellowtail lugworm and is also affected by season, temperature, wind and the state of the tide. In some regions during the winter both types of lugworm can be deeper than two spits, and digging them requires skill and stamina. In most cases the yellowtail lugworm can only be dug one at a time by targeting individual worms.

In some regions water on the sand can hamper digging. Here you will need to dig a moat to drain off the excess sea water. The trick is to use the wind direction to drain off the water. A small half moon-shaped moat is a worthwhile consideration when waterlogged sand is a problem.

All worm digging techniques rely on digging a clean hole, with lots of small forkfuls of ground far more efficient than large ones. The best system entails using the fork so that it is only cutting through two edges of the sand with each forkful. The technique takes some getting used to, but is the most efficient, so take the time

to watch an experienced digger if you can. The novice who tries to pull the fork through three of the squares of sand each dig risks breaking his fork or his back! As you dig lugworm, put them into a bucket of clean sea water. This will enable them to purge themselves of sand. Beware of grabbing heads and tails of worms – they break. Better to take another spit out of the sand and expose the worm fully. Cut or damaged worms are best kept separate from whole worms because the leaking blood will kill them. When you finish digging, carefully wash the worms free of sand. Rinse them a couple of times in clean sea water and then, if your are using them within a few days, wrap common lugworm in several layers of clean newspaper. Yellowtails can be kept in fresh, clean seawater, while black lugworm are best wrapped singly in dry newspaper. Do not handle worms excessively, and that includes continually unwrapping them for a look.

Separation is an important topic when collecting the different baits. Damaged and whole worms should be kept apart, while some baits are best kept in water, others out of it. A nest of buckets is a great idea, and although there are not any commercially-available bait digging bucket kits yet, it is comparatively easy to collect a range of buckets that slot into one another. A lid can also be a good idea, because more than one nest of buckets has spilled in the car boot!

A nest of buckets with water in the base bucket also makes a good cooling system in summer to keep bait alive while you dig. A good idea is a small clip-on container on the side of the bucket for split or cut worms, or for small white ragworm and the like.

LUGWORM DIGGING TIPS

- Stand back and survey the sand (below) before you start digging common lugworm, and look for a concentration of worms. Lugworm tend to space themselves out in sand, so you rarely dig lots together, although moving between the densest groups is often more productive than digging at random or blind.

- In many regions you can dig small white ragworm among lugworm. Put these in a small container of water and not in with the lugworm (below).

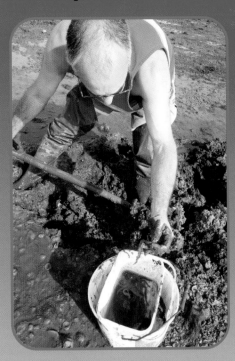

- Cut, split and damaged worms are worth keeping, because they will start to deteriorate as soon as they are killed. This gives them a different scent and feel to your live worms, and sometimes this scent can be deadly.

- Never grap a worm by the tail, take another spit from the sand with the fork to expose the whole worm.

"Pumping lugworm requires just as much skill and effort as digging them with a spade"

PUMPING LUGWORM

Pumping lugworms is a comparatively new technique in the UK, and it has grown in popularity over digging the yellowtail lugworms with a small spade. Worms are targeted individually by placing the pump over the worm cast, or at an angle close to it. The Australians have been using bait pumps for decades, and they have been in the UK for a long time. However, most people ignored their potential until it was discovered that a smaller bore worked efficiently for yellowtail lugworm. In some regions the larger blow lugworm can also be sucked from the sand with a pump. The downside of a worm pump is that it often damages the worms, and in some cases the worm is killed by the pump but not extracted. Some professional pumpers use washing-up liquid to enhance their pumps, and this has had a detrimental effect on worm beds.

Most of the commercial worm pumps have a large diameter/bore that requires a gorilla to operate. The professionals use home-made 25-30mm bore pumps.

If you know a friendly plumber, persuade him to make you one up – they are simple enough, just a coupe of tap washers in a tube with a central rod and handle.

When they work, worm pumps are ridiculously easy, almost criminally so, and some may feel guilty at the ease with which your bucket fills with lugworm. At other times you feel as if you should get a free boomerang with each worm, they are that deep!

The secret to it all is accurate precise pumping. You need to generate suction in the worm's burrow – cut across the burrow and all is lost. Wind direction, atmospheric pressure, the state of the tide and the dampness of the sand all affect the technique, but once learned it is far less tedious than a spade, and you can pump left or right-handed. The only drawback in terms of the worms is that it does stress yellowtails so that they burst. Fully gut the worms and then wrap or roll them in clean, dry newspaper.

- Spade diggers cannot get at worms in pools, whereas the water in a pool increases the suction of the bigger-bore pumps, making them work more efficiently.

- The suction of most pumps tends to drag them further into the sand. This means a pump will cut the burrow and the worm. The technique is to suck the worm up to the pump, not the pump down to the worm.

- Pumped worms should be put in a dry bucket and washed later – put in water they become washed-out. Make sure you fully gut worms before wrapping. If any blood or juices are left, this tends to make the worm go soft.

"There is a wing nut in the end of the pump which adjusts the pressure"

DIGGING KING RAGWORM

King ragworm are dug randomly in most cases, although the bigger worms can be targeted individually by looking for their water spurt and chasing them down their brown burrow. It's mostly about finding a patch with the most worms in it, and a clue to this is to look for stones and rocks that other diggers have avoided. Ragworm digging can be messy because the mud on occasions is foul-smelling – not for the faint-hearted or those on the way to the office. Essential equipment is a lightweight fork with thin, round tines. These are easy to wriggle around and penetrate stony ground. A pair of waders helps to keep the mud off your clothes.

"Finish the digging session by washing off mud and sand from bucket, fork and waders"

"There are two types of ragworm popular with sea anglers – the largest king ragworm and the smaller white ragworm"

Dig your ragworm into a bucket of sea water. As with lugworm, this allows them to clean themselves of the mud they have ingested as they burrow. Rinse them in clean sea water when you have finished digging. Worms can then be put into a tray lined with newspaper in damp sea peat, or wrapped in small packets in sea peat. Some shops supply ragworm in vermiculite insulation material, but this tends to dry the worms out quickly.

Another medium for storing ragworm in is popper seaweed. Dry the weed and lay it on several layers of newspaper in a tray, then place the washed ragworm on top. When they have worked their way to the bottom of the weed, replace the newspaper and turn the weed over. This system keeps them fresh for several days.

"Wash, drain and remove mud and sand from worms before you leave"

Ragworm digging tips

- Pick worms up with one hand only. Keep the hand driving the fork clean, and never wash your hands as you dig. It's a recipe for blisters!

- When digging in thick mud, take along a large bath sponge. It's great for washing mud off waders, forks, buckets and you.

- Heavy footfalls and standing on the spot you are about to dig can push worms deeper. Dig with one foot in the hole you are excavating.

- A coarse fishing maggot riddle is perfect for washing small ragworm and maddies free of mud.

- Digging worms when the sand is totally drained at dead low water and as the tide returns is generally more productive.

- The less glossy newspaper etc are better for rapping worms because they absorb the water. Use glossy paper and the worms cannot dry out.

"Always replace rocks how you found them. Scattering rocks can ruin the habitat of other marine creatures"

COLLECTING YOUR OWN PEELER CRABS

To determine whether a crab is a peeler, simply pull off the end leg segment, which should reveal an identical soft, new leg. If just a white sinew is exposed it is not a peeler. Crabs in an advanced state of shedding their shell will have cracks around the back of the shell, and sometimes you find crabs halfway out of their shell, or completely jelly-soft. The test of a perfect peeler ready for the hook is that it is coming out of its shell and you can crush the shell or a claw between finger and thumb.

Shore crabs peel at different times of the year as water and sea temperatures rise. The common shore crab is the first to shed, followed by spider and edible crabs and finally velvet swimmers. Where and when to find peeling crabs depends on your location – indeed, some regions, notably the South West estuaries, are blessed with an early flush and an almost continuous year-round supply where the warmth of the Gulf Stream prompts the common shore crab to peel regularly, even throughout the winter.

The peak peeler season for the rest of the UK starts in April in the South and ends in August in the North. Weather plays a big part: crabs can peel out in deep water if the weather is not favourable, or else the season can be prolonged inshore.

In recent years this has happened as a result of an extended summer – some say global warming. A long spell of hot weather can hurry along the peeling season, heavy rain can curtail it, while cool weather can prolong it.

Some regions have few peeling crabs on the shore at all because they peel offshore. This tends to be the case with the open beaches that face the Atlantic Ocean and North Sea. However all the river estuaries, mud flats, salty backwaters and most sheltered shores have rocks, groynes, pools, holes and mud, as well as sea weed, for the crabs to hide in. If you choose to go crabbing in places offering one or more of these features, you won't go far wrong. Avoid dramatic storm shores and deep-water regions that are subject to heavy seas!

To be a crabber in some regions you need to be brave. Crabs will hide anywhere that affords them shelter, and it's just amazing how high up the tide line they will venture and the kinds of places they will seek out. Shake the sea weed hanging from the harbour wall or jetty supports and that will open your eyes to the endless possibilities. What looks a pretty plain and uncomplicated shoreline can harbour lots of places where crabs will hide, yet many anglers do not ever realise they are there!

CRABBING TIPS

- Shedding crabs need sea water for support when they shed their shell. If you want to collect crabs for use immediately, look under weed in pools.

- Where a large volume of sea weed is washed or blown inshore by the wind, crabs can be collected after dark with a lamp as they sit on top of the weed, but move carefully. In daylight you can trawl your arms through the weed to locate crabs.

"Purpose-made peeler crab traps are laid in many estuaries. Old tyres, drainpipes and guttering all attract crabs"

In estuaries the deep mud retains its temperature. This can prolong the peeling season, and invariably this is the place to produce peelers. As a starting point, look in the corners of the groyne posts – dig deep in the mud here and also check both sides of the groyne, up the planking and amid clusters of mussel shells. Any rock, ledge, tile, brick or slab is worth feeling around. Old tyres are perfect crab habitats and if you come across one, check out the inside. Even the tiniest stone can have a peeler under it, and when searching under rocks, don't forget to feel in the mud underneath. Many peelers escape detection here!

Rocks in pools are the perfect place to look for peelers that are in prime condition to use on the hook – that's because crabs need the support water or mud gives them when they shed.
A peeled crab takes on loads of water to pump itself up to its new size and then harden. When you lift a rock, the crab will always scuttle back under it, often unseen – so feel around the base of the rock. Replacing it carefully means you can always check it again later.

Next...dare you put your arm up to the elbow down a river estuary rat hole? Have you got the bottle to get on your hands and knees and poke about down to your shoulder in rocky holes, or mud, or slimy weed? You could surprise an eel or a powerful edible crab, or encounter the pincers of an irate lobster, although these are generally found further down the tide line in summer when edible peelers are the target! Peelers become less aggressive the further they get into the process, but crabs in the early stages, especially cock crabs, can nip – so watch those fingers! The real crabbing dangers are broken bottles, shells, sharp flints and barnacles. Try a chainmail filleting glove if you are into delving deep.

Wimps might opt for the rocks – lifting rocks in pools is easy, until you find a back-busting boulder. But don't despair if you can't lift it. Either get a mate to help you and share the proceeds, or, if you want the crab haul for yourself, the trick is to stand legs akimbo and rock the rock backwards and forwards. Crabs will scuttle in all directions, but you have to be quick to catch them.

The big plus of crabbing is that you can do it every tide. Unlike worms, which take longer to re-populate an area, crabs come inshore and shuffle between hiding places every tide. It may pay to visit your spot as early in the tide as possible if your venue is popular. If it's not, then setting up a few crab traps of your own could prove worthwhile.

Put your collected crabs in a bucket with clean sea weed, regularly drain away any water, and segregate the soft crabs and peelers.

COLLECTING SHELLFISH
Most of the shellfish used by sea anglers produce the best results when they are being washed up by heavy seas. At such times it is easy for the angler to visit the venue as the tide floods to pick up a supply. Often, on storm-exposed coasts, you can collect shellfish at low water, but this is only possible when a spring low tide coincides with an onshore gale which smashes inshore sand bars apart and spews marine life inshore.

Razorfish
Dig or collect these at the extremes of low tide. An effective method is to look for the small keyhole-shaped entrance to the razor's burrow and pour a concentrated salt water liquid down it. Use a washing up liquid bottle and the razor will pop up like magic to the surface. You can also dig razorfish with a small spade or fork, but you need to be quick.

Piddock clams
These are found in clay and chalk rock regions, where they can be dug with a fork or a small pick.

"Hen crabs have a curved abdomen and cock crabs have a pointed abdomen. This hen is a soft crab, having already peeled"

"Peeler crabs are less aggresive when they are peeling, because their pincers lack any power – but when crabbing beware of non-peelers!"

"Spreading your worms through a series of trays inside your bait fridge will keep them healthy indefinitely"

The ability to keep a constant supply of baits fresh and alive is a big advantage for the sea angler, especially since not all baits are available to dig or buy every day of the week or throughout the year. The height of the tide, the weather and the season all affect their collection, especially in the depths of winter, when snow water and freezing temperatures – not to mention neap tides – can make worm digging virtually impossible.

Essential to any bait supply is a fridge...not the one in the kitchen if you value your marriage or family! An old domestic fridge freezer in the garage is ideal for the average sea angler as a compact storage system for frozen and live baits. A more advanced system can include a water pump to circulate sea water through a series of trays arranged cascade-style. This can be complicated to set up, but a few of the UK's top anglers do employ an elaborate marine fridge. The larger cooler fridges used in pubs and clubs, with a clear door and lots of shelves, are ideal for the bait fanatic and can be picked up fairly cheaply from fridge repairs firm. Other options include a small caravan fridge. The advantage here is that it can be taken with you – many a match angler rolls into a hotel with his own bait fridge!

Whatever your fridge choice, it is an essential for the serious sea angler. You can store live baits in shallow cat litter trays stacked on the shelves. Store worms in a small amount of water, just a dribble, to keep them wet. Deep water allows bacteria to travel quickly between worms. Lugworm and ragworm will keep fresh and alive for a week or more in a small amount of sea water. Some anglers use coral sand to help maintain a bacteria-free tank system, and coal dust has a similar anti-bacterial property. Both are ideal if you want to transport worms like white ragworm by car, because the worms can bury in the sand and not be slopped about or damaged. Always check worms in the fridge regularly, and remove any dead or damaged individuals. Replace water if it becomes coloured, from a bottle of fresh water kept in the fridge so it is at the same temperature.

Crabs can be segregated by their state of peel. Those coming out of their shells are most difficult to keep alive. Store them in damp tissue or newspaper and do not give them any water, as this will merely speed up their shedding. Store them in the coldest part of the fridge. Crabs for use should also be stored in wet tissue and can be encouraged to shed by watering them regularly. A garden spray of sea water, kept inside the fridge, is ideal. Store your ready supply in the bottom of the fridge.

Crabs in the initial stage of shedding are best kept out of the fridge in a bucket or cool box. Water them regularly and remove any that start to show signs of peeling to the fridge. By keeping tabs on your crabs as they go through the peeling process you can collect a supply for each future fishing session, or to freeze. Live peelers can be hard to obtain in winter, and lots of anglers with a supply of frozen crabs make a killing at that time of year.

COOL BOXES AND BAGS

Cool boxes are equally effective in winter and summer for keeping baits alive and fresh during a fishing session, bearing in mind that surplus bait kept alive can be saved for next time. Add a couple of freezer packs to the bag or box if you are travelling, and beware of packing bait in the rear of the car in summer in hot weather without some form of cooling.

Cool bags are easiest to pack in your tackle box or bucket if you have a long walk to your venue.

BAIT STORAGE TIPS

- Bait trays that slot inside each other maximise room in your bait fridge.

- Don't pile newspaper packets of worms on top of one another in the fridge. Seal them inside a plastic bag. This stops the newspaper getting damp, which can kill or ruin lugworm.

- Wide-necked stainless steel food flasks are perfect for storing frozen baits.

- Store a spare supply of sea water in a lidded bucket in a dark cupboard. That way, any bacteria will die and the sediment will settle.

- In winter a line of peat (it looks like tea leaves) is deposited on many shorelines. This is sea peat – winter's dead leaves, twigs, bark and seaweed – which is the perfect medium for storing ragworm and maddies. It is also ideal as a filter material to keep the circulated water in a tanking system clean.

- When you go fishing, don't spread all your bait out in one go in the sun, rain or wind. All these extremes of weather will soon kill or ruin live baits. Keep some back, wrapped in newspaper or in a cool box, for use later.

- Beware of handling live bait excessively, resit the temptation to keep disturbing worms etc.

- In summer a half full bottle of drinking water can be frozen and used as a cool pack in your cool bag to keep bait alive, once it thaws it can be used to quench your thirst.

CHAPTER 7
CASTING

Beachcasting destroys the myth that sea angling is not physical, energetic or sportingly skilled. Yet this myth continues to be believed by the novice angler, who arrives with a beachcaster on a winter shoreline – it can all be a horrendous shock if the wind is blowing. Would you attempt a full-sized golf course as a total novice golfer without a single lesson? Of course not – so the first piece of advice for the total beginner is to get casting lessons, because throwing money at the best fishing tackle is only a small part of the solution.

Distance casting has been hyped up over the years, and some of the elite casters may be to blame for making even their practical casting distances seem out of the reach of mere mortals. The truth is that modern tackle, like golf clubs, has evolved, and is a great equaliser for increasing casting performance. However, a rod and reel alone will not do the job for you and no amount of money will put yards on your ability, but a suitable outfit can ensure that you start on the right foot and will be able to perform to your potential. Beware of being outgunned by tournament hype and tackle that makes it appear that all you need is a powerful rod. You still need the shoulders and the skill to get the best from it. Liken a rod to a bow and arrow: If you cannot pull the string back, the arrow goes nowhere; if the string is sloppy and easy to pull back, its potential is limited. What you want is a rod that you can bend and get the most from.
As for accuracy, that is another problem for most with the loss of accuracy in terms of direction proportional to the power input.

Let's look at practical casting distances – tournament distances have extended past 300 metres in recent times, but these distances are obtained only by a few top casters using a plain lead with a following wind and no bait. They have precious little in common with the real world. However, some proficient casters can put a baited hook close to or over the 200 metre mark. Most untutored novices can't make 80 metres at their first attempt.

Distances that fish can be caught at are between a few metres and hundreds of metres, and while in most cases a good cast (100-plus metres) will put you among fish, on occasions some species will be almost close enough to touch.
Using casting to your advantage includes knowing when to cast short or long, as well as controlling an ego that wants to show others how good a caster you are!

Being able to cast more than 100 metres is a big advantage, especially in winter when weather conditions are severe. Powering a heavy lead (175 grams) into a head wind and past the turmoil of the surf enables you to continue fishing in the worst conditions.

"Greater distances are produced when the rod is powered to its maximum"

Top Tip – A caster capable of reaching long distances can always chose to drop his bait short.
A caster lacking distance has no choice but to fish in the gutter.
Casting lessons and practice will ultimately improve results, but beware of a casting ego!

This is when all the hard work and practice pays off, because all around you those with cheap tackle and an unpractised technique will struggle to put a bait far enough out for it to stay there.

Casting trajectory is an important consideration, depending on the conditions. With a following wind a high trajectory will catch the wind and a few metres can be added to a cast. In a gale, however, a low trajectory helps to punch the lead and bait through the wind.

As a last resort, a sensible choice of venue is always a way around a lack of casting distance. Piers, deep harbours, headlands and rough ground are all venues that will produce fish to a shorter cast. It can, though, be a mistake to select your venue with a following wind purely to increase casting distance. As a general rule of thumb, the best fishing is most often to be had when casting into the wind.

SHOCK LEADER and KNOTS

It is worth repeating the important role played by shock leaders in shore casting. The consequences of leads between 4oz and 8oz snapping the line and flying off in all directions are horrendous to contemplate, and for that reason a casting shock leader is essential for all types of shore casting.

The formula for working out the minimum breaking strain of the leader is simply. For each ounce of lead, use 10lb of breaking strain. 5oz = 50lb shock leader; 6oz = 60lb shock leader, and so on. For rough weather, field casting or when using leads over 5oz, add another 10lb to the shock leader breaking strain for extra safety.

Your shock leader needs to be long enough to go around the reel spool six times, and the length of the drop should be from rod tip to lead plus the length of the rod. An extra metre allows for cutting the end of the leader off to tie on rig connectors and suchlike.

As a rough guide, five times the distance between your two outstretched hands is the length to aim for. Remember to continue the leader strength through your rig.

Check leaders and knots for damage regularly, and treat every cast as if your life depended on it, especially on crowded venues, because someone else's could!

Uni Leader Knot

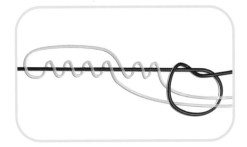

The easiest and quickest shock leader knot to tie is the Uni knot. Originally developed by tournament casters, this knot is small and unobtrusive but is not suited for rough ground.

"The Uni leader knot is small and neat but not so strong"

"You need to bend a rod to get the best response from it. If you cannot bend the rod casting distance will be drastically reduced"

Tapered leaders

Tapered shock leaders are available in a range of sizes, standard is 60lb down to 15lb. Lighter carp leaders are also available from 30lb down to 12lb etc and these have their uses in light line conditions. Always consider the line strength/weight of the lead ratio when selecting the breaking strain of a tapered shock leader. They are particularly suitable for use with level line multipliers that have a small line guide and can also be used as a quick replacement leader if one is lost whilst you are fishing, or if fishing a weedy sea when weed is causing a standard leader knot to clog and jam in the tip ring.

A tapered leader allows the use of a smaller sized knot with the standard blood knot suitable for joining lines of equal diameter and this is more efficient on fixed spool reels where a large leader knot can jam and pull coils of line off the spool.

Shock leader knots

There are three shock leader knots that are popular for power casting and fishing. Unfortunately over the years the trend towards the smallest knot has been promoted by field casters and these are not necessarily the strongest. In recent years the Bimini Twist leader knot has grown in popularity amongst anglers and although long and bulky it is superior in strength to all other mono leader joints. The Bimini originated as a big game knot for joining different diameter lines and has been adapted by the UK beach angler.

The essence of the Bimini is that it is a long knot which allows the knot to stretch when under strain thus spreading the pressure over the length of the knot and not on a small area of the lowest diameter line.

The Bimini is the ultimate leader knot for all round fishing including the roughest venues.

When tying any knot in monofilament lines pull the knot together gently and gradually wetting the line as you go. Mono will scar and burn if pulled into a knot too rapidly.

The Bimini twist loop is tied in the main line with the number of twists effecting the eventual length, 20 to 30 twists produce a practical knot for beachcasting.

A favourite leader knot is the Uni knot which is the one that came from the tournament field. It is strong enough for fishing from clean ground but not so good for rough ground. First form a single overhand knot in the leader line. Pass the main line through the loop, twist six times around the leader and then pass back through the loop and tease tight. A variation is to turn the mainline back around the leader material another six times inside the loop it forms with the first six turns before passing it back through the loop and this is the strongest variation. Trim and blob the ends with a lighter flame.

The third knot is the Blood knot and this is only recommended for lines of equal diameter as in the joint between main line and a tapered leader.

This knot is small and strong and easy to tie on the beach. Wrap the two lines together eight turns and pass each end through the centre loop of those turns -tease tight and trim off the ends.

"The Bimini leader knot is bulky but is the strongest leader joint"

Shock Leader Knot (bimini)

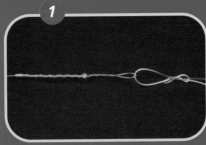

1. The shock leader is tied to the bimini loop via a two turn grinner knot.

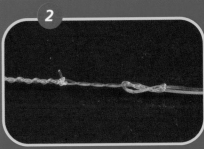

2. Once the grinner knot is tied in the loop pull it tight slowly and the knot will form and lock into the loop.

3. Trim lose ends of the knot with clippers and finish the knot by melting (blob) the mono ends with a lighter.

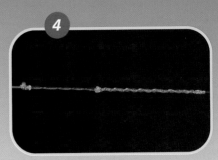

4. The finished knot.
(The complete bimini loop and knot is shown in more detail on page 79)

Please take care with this stage. This procedure should not be attempted by children under the age of 16 unless supervised by an adult.

There are a number of casting styles and in all cases the power input relates directly to the distance achieved. I won't dwell too long on this subject because words alone can never replace a practical casting lesson. This puts you in the hands of an expert, who will not only show you the technique, but ensure your tackle set-up matches your physique and ability.

Your height, physique and power all affects your casting potential, although co-ordination and timing are often equally important. There is also a degree of thought that needs to go into the practical side of casting. Stance and room on the beach, any obstacles to avoid, where the wind is coming from, what tackle and bait size will be most suitable – to reach optimum distances you will need to get everything right.

POWER PENDULUM
At the top of the distance ratings is the power pendulum, which is a critically timed power cast involving swinging the lead in a wide arc to increase initial compression in the rod. Timing and power are important in this cast and, like the best golf swing, not all can reach this standard. Pendulum rods tend to be stiff, with most of the action in the tip third of the rod.

The style came from the casting tournament field, where it is flat grass with plenty of room. Therefore the drop (length of line) between the rod tip and the lead can be long – this increases rod compression when the lead is swung in an exaggerated pendulum arc. Unfortunately, on the shore, such an exaggerated drop and swing are rarely possible so the style has to be modified somewhat. Most anglers prefer what is called a 'mini pendulum' or 'beach pendulum' style. The length of the drop is shortened and the pendulum swing curtailed. This stubby pendulum style can still prove very effective and is reasonably safe in most cases, although any form of pendulum cast on a crowded venue is not recommended. Casting is all about common sense – beware of those who take tournament styles on to the beach or pier. It is irresponsible and dangerous!

You can make the pendulum cast with the reel in the high or low position, although the low position and a long rod is by far the more efficient and easier to handle. This is because the lead moves in a wide arc during the cast and travels more slowly, making casting timing less critical and easy to control. With the reel in the high

position the lead speed is much faster, because of the smaller arc, and here the timing is everything.

Most anglers chose the multiplier for pendulum casting, although it is possible to use a high or low position fixed-spool reel for this style. With a fixed-spool reel a line release mechanism is easier to use than your finger. An alternative is a finger stall, or you can hold the reel above the rod and use your thumb to grip the line.

BACK CAST
This is the preferred style of some anglers to combat bad weather and to gain maximum distance with a heavy lead or bulky bait load. A pendulum rod is suitable, but in most cases back cast models have a reinforced, stiffer butt section. The back cast involves the pendulum style, but as the name suggests the angler uses his whole body and casts with his back to the sea. This is the most athletic style used by anglers. Very long drops, tip to lead, are used in this style and it's similar to that used for throwing the hammer, but without the spins! It is a very effective power style for throwing leads of up to 10oz into the teeth of a gale, and still the preferred style on shallow coasts like Norfolk, where distance casting is essential.

OFF THE GROUND
The OTG (off the ground) cast is a far more controlled, accurate and smooth cast than the others, and produces some very good distances with bait. Timing is important, but less of a problem to master than with the pendulum, and most novices find this an easy starting point. There are many variations on this casting style, which launches the lead from a standing start. It originated from the layback which, as its name suggests, involves using the body like a coiled spring to increase arm power. Again, this style is suitable for multiplier or fixed-spool reels. Most casters find the low reel position with a multiplier superior in terms of distance, accuracy and handling.

OVERHEAD THUMP
The overhead thump is the most basic style used by lots of novices without any coaching at all - it's like throwing a stone and it comes naturally. This is the easiest style for the novice to master, and it is by far the best for accuracy of direction and distance. This is why it has become such a favourite with certain match anglers. In all cases the correct and balanced tackle is paramount for attaining the maximum distance, the marriage of reel size

and rod length being critical. In recent years longer, lighter rods and braid lines have increased the distance potential of this style, simply because a longer rod means a longer lever. In the past, overhead casters progressed to the off the ground or pendulum style with time and experience to increase their distance, but nowadays, with advances in tackle design, casting overhead is almost on a par with the pendulum in terms of distance, but without the dangers involved in that style.

It's essential when choosing tackle to remember that you can be overpowered by too great a rod length and weight. Just as a pendulum rod can be too stiff for the angler to bend, an over-long rod can be too heavy for the caster to move through the casting stroke with any speed!

FIXED-SPOOL CASTING
In the past the multiplier has always been superior in terms of casting distance, but the lighter carbon rod-building materials have allowed longer rods to be produced, and these have favoured the OTG or overhead thump styles used by fixed-spool casters, especially novices. The fixed-spool is still considered the novice reel because it is almost foolproof in use. However, it too has advanced in recent times, with coned spools and superb level line lay. This has made it popular with more experienced anglers because of the ease with which accurate long-distance casts can be made. Its retrieve is also faster than that of the multiplier because the spool diameter does not reduce significantly after casting, as it does with the multiplier. Initial line retrieval, a vital consideration when fishing rough ground, can be made at a faster rate from the outset, whereas a multiplier spool needs to fill before it gets to top speed!

Distances with a multiplier and a fixed-spool reel are very much on a par, although it's easier for the novice to master the fixed-spool and obtain a reasonable distance, and the fixed-spool performs best in calm, still conditions. Fixed-spool reels are more suitable for light lines, while the multiplier has a narrow band of diameters that it can handle efficiently
You can only use braided line with a fixed-spool reel for shore casting. On a multiplier the coils jam into one another, and casting becomes a problem.

"Sea Angler magazine editor Mel Russ in full back cast"

"*Many believe the multiplier reel to be more efficient for general and long range fishing in the UK*"

MULTIPLIER CASTING

The multiplier reel is considered by many as more efficient for long-range fishing over clean ground, and it is easier for the average angler to reach greater distances with a multiplier than a fixed-spool, especially with large baits and heavy leads and in the worst UK conditions. A multiplier sits on the rod and is balanced, while the fixed-spool is seen by some as gawky.

Multipliers are more difficult to control on the cast – although modern brakes have eased the overrun problem, it still exists. You still have to thumb and slow the spool when the lead hits the water. This is something many novices find difficult to judge.

Also essential to the multiplier's performance is the way the line is laid on the spool. A thumb-driven cotton reel line lay encourages a smooth release of the line during the cast, but this takes practice. An integral line lay mechanism on reels cuts distance drastically.

It would seem that the multiplier has little going for it, and yet the majority of experienced UK sea anglers still choose this type of reel.

MULTIPLIER TIP

- The larger model multipliers suitable for rock fishing are not so efficient for long-range casting. Always match the line diameter to the spool capacity for the best performance.

OVERRUNS

Overruns and the resultant monofilament hedgehog with a multiplier reel are the consequence of reels being overloaded with line, the wrong diameter line, a mistimed cast, an uneven line lay, knots, haste, or a lack of tension in the line as it is retrieved. However, in recent years multipliers with fibre and magnetic brakes have almost eradicated this problem. A quality multiplier with these features is the key to avoiding the dreaded birds nest. Do not overload the spool with line, and ensure that the brakes are deployed. Smooth casting is also assisted by balanced tackle and bait.

Most anglers will experience an overrun, sooner or later, and it's a good idea to carry a spare reel if you use a multiplier. With a fixed-spool reel tangles are rare, and you can always change the spool easily if line is lost or snapped.

"The birds nest (above) is caused by a variety of reasons, although in most cases it's due to human error."

- Lots of anglers are unwilling to practise their casting without fishing. A few lessons from a casting instructor or even a fellow angler can be invaluable, and will at least set you off in the correct direction and give you some idea of the tackle's set-up and potential.

- Check that line is not wrapped around your rod tip or intermediate ring before casting. This is a common cause of snaps-offs on the beach.

- Rod action changes when a baited rig is clipped on to the line. Lots of rods have been designed to cast just a lead a long way, but the hype that sells them doesn't tell you this. Bait and tackle can often overpower a beachcaster's action, and this is particularly noticeable with many of the low-grade carbon composite economy rods!

- A word of caution on long rods – the cheaper rods made of a heavier grade carbon will not perform to the same standard as the lighter, more expensive types. Beware of long rods that are over-heavy.

- The off-the-ground cast can cause bait clips to come adrift prior to casting. Add a tension spring to the top snood of your rig to prevent this. (below)

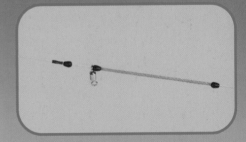

- A section of a rubber glove finger (thumby) on your thumb allows far more spool grip, and is handy for wet weather or field casting.

WHERE CAN I FIND AN INSTRUCTOR?

Around the country there are lots of casting clubs and casting instructors. Some give their time free through the local angling club, others charge for tuition. Check out your local club or tackle shop.

Sea Angler Magazine has a countrywide list of casting instructors. To find the nearest instructor in your area, contact: Sea Angler Magazine at www.seaangler.co.uk

I am not a fan of messing around with my multipliers – I tend to give them a clean-out and oiling ever four months or so. This involves disassembling them via the two or three-screw take apart, wiping them out with an oily cloth and re-oiling the bearings with the oil supplied with the reel. Fixed-spool reels require little maintenance, if any.

Tournament techniques of removing grease and installing special grade oils in multipliers is not required for fishing, and most anglers merely do damage to their reels by stripping them of grease. There is no salt in a field, but at sea salt water is highly corrosive. If your reel lets you down because you have taken away that protective internal layer of grease and oil, don't run moaning to the manufacturer!

A regular wash and brush with an old toothbrush under the warm tap to clean off salt and grime after every trip is all that is needed. Add a little shampoo if the crud is thick.

Draining the reel and leaving it to dry thoroughly is very important – leave wet reels in bags inside a tackle box for three weeks and they will corrode, so give them some air.

Tuning a multiplier is a less complicated process than many think. Some multipliers have a spool float control each side, others just the one on the handle side. Simply screw down the end float adjustment until the spool has no lateral movement, then loosen off one half-turn. On most reels this will adjust the spool perfectly, and with practice you will learn what adjustment best suits your reel.

Some models run better if the spool has more lateral movement, and it is a fact that there can be a lot of performance difference between multipliers of the same model.

Magnetic brakes have been a great step forward in casting control, and tuning them is fairly simple. First cast, push the control full on, and then loosen it off once the line is wet and bedded in.

If you are in doubt about taking a reel apart, or have a problem with your reel, most of the manufacturers have a service department. Box your reel securely and send it recorded delivery with an explanatory letter detailing your problem.

"The sea environment is tough on tackle, buy the best and keep it in top condition, it won't let you down"

CHAPTER 8
SAFETY, CONSERVATION AND RULES

S ea angling involves getting close to some very dangerous items – sharp hooks, knives, fish teeth, and some pretty obnoxious mud, slime and baits.

Take care with sharp hooks, and don't hold a hook in your teeth when tying it to the line – the consequences could be an embarrassing trip to the hospital or a doctor. Always cut bait by running the knife away from your fingers. Scissors can be safer.

Be extra careful of sharp teeth and spines when manhandling big fish like shark, sting ray or bass for the camera. A filleting glove is ideal for unhooking and fish handling, as well as filleting and crabbing.

Be especially careful when unhooking fish. Lots of fin and gill spines will be germ-laden, so it's good advice to clean any wound and keep an eye on it.

Having been hospitalised by an unknown virus, I can warn from bitter experience that eating your sandwiches with muddy hands can be very unwise.

A small first aid kit in your tackle box is a good idea. All it needs is various sizes of sticking plaster, a finger stall (which also comes in handy for casting), and a roll of plastic or PVC tape. This can be useful when you cut a finger in an awkward place where a plaster will not stick because your hands are wet.

The BBC shipping and inshore waters forecasts are the most reliable for the sea angler. Wind speed over the sea is faster than over the land, and land-based forecasts such as those from your local TV weather girl can be way out in terms of the time of arrival of a weather front. Expecting the worst possible scenario is the safest bet if you are going to a remote or exposed venue, especially at night in winter.

The shipping forecasts are for the next 24 hours, which is a good safety margin for boat anglers, but shore anglers will find them useful, too.

While the modern forecast is usually very accurate, there are a number of old sayings that ring true in terms of weather prediction. Favourites are 'Red sky at night, shepherd's delight' and 'Red sky in the morning, shepherd's warning'.
Take notice of these two, because they are seldom wrong.

Wind strength or force is a good guide to the weather, with any wind blowing onshore under a force six likely to produce good fishing. Stronger than a force six onshore and you will struggle to fish – over force eight and fishing is almost impossible. Then is the time to look for a leeward shore. Wind direction is always given as the direction the wind is coming from, in other words, a west wind comes from the west.

The Beaufort scale is used to gauge wind strength – here is a shortened version

Force 1 – Light air, ripples, wind speed 1-3 knots

Force 2 – Light breeze, small waves, 4-6 knots

Force 3 – Gentle breeze large wavelets, some crests, 7-10 knots

Force 4 – Moderate breeze, small waves, some white horses, 11-16 knots

Force 5 – Fresh breeze, moderate, fairly long waves, white horses, some spray, 17-21 knots

Force 6 – Strong breeze, some large waves, foaming, wave crests and spray, 22-27 knots

Force 7 – Near gale, large swells, wave crests producing foam and spray, 28-33 knots

Force 8 – Gale, long, high waves, crests breaking into foam and streaks, 34-40 knots.

Force 9 – Strong gale, high waves, dense foam, visibility difficult through spray, 41-47 knots

*A knot is one nautical mile per hour

Weather tips

- Lightning poses a danger to anglers because carbon beachcasters are a good conductor of electricity so avoid being on an open beach near the sea in a lightening storm. One of the safest places is your car.

- Air pressure can be measured with a barometer. A rapid change in pressure usual indicates deterioration in the weather, rising pressure is usually associated with improving weather, although it can also indicate a surge of cold air, rain, snow or storms.

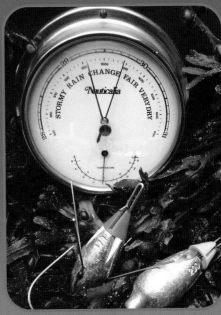

- The most efficient way to keep dry when fishing in the open in a situation where a shelter cannot be used is to wear "Geordie Pyjamas". Chest waders are the perfect answer to prolonged torrential rain, linked to a good waterproof top or smock they allow you to fish, even sit down, without getting wet. For rough ground and weed insure your chesties have studded soles. Most waterproof suits loose their waterproofing when washed in a washing machine.

CONSERVATION

Catch and release is growing in popularity among sea anglers, and although conservation is the buzz word, the ability to take a picture of your catch with your mobile phone has completely solved the problem of others not believing what you have caught.

Sea fish are still very much a target for the table, and long may they be so. How many members of the public have tasted a mackerel fried straight from the sea, rather than the grey-eyed, pappy supermarket samples which are not even good enough for bait? Take what you want and no more – a good policy is to release the bigger fish. These are the established breeders. It is better to kill a tiddler that has yet to run the gauntlet of nets, predators and anglers.

In time, catch limits per species will be imposed on UK sea anglers and many of the conservation issues that anglers want will become fact.

INSURANCE

Some form of third party public liability insurance is essential for the angler, and this is why it is advisable to join an angling club. Most angling clubs and organisations offer a third party public liability scheme as a part of membership. The purpose of this is to protect members, especially club officials, from being sued in the case of liability after an accident. Should you be involved in an accident you are then protected. You can obtain similar public liability cover via your house insurance to include your tackle, but this may be considerably more expensive.

"Are you covered?
Public liability insurance is an
essential for power casters"

Returning fish after the hook has been removed is simply a matter of slipping them back into the water gently and as soon as possible. However, there are a range of potential problems, such as a long drop to the water when fishing from piers or cliffs. Some species are more delicate than others, and the size of the fish makes a big difference to its potential survival. You can use a drop net or bucket to lower fish back from a height, although some anglers simply drop the fish head-first from as close a point to the water they can. An alternative with smaller fish is to hang them on the wire of the grip lead and lower it. Placing a small fish in a bucket of sea water, allowing it time to recover before returning it, can also improve the survival rate.

Careless handling of fish is a major cause of casualties. Many of the delicate species like pollack, pout and cod lose scales and slime, and are prone to being dropped when they wriggle. A wet cloth is generally recommended for handling fish, although many anglers consider it better not to handle small fish at all if possible.

Some species can be held by the mouth causing less damage to their flanks, while hanging them from the hook snood is a better alternative than gripping their body. Dogfish, smoothhound and rays are tougher and can be handled, but it may then be you that is in danger from sandpaper skin, thorns and spines.

Hook damage is another major cause of fish fatality, some species being more prone than others to dying from being hooked deeply. Flatfish rarely survive a soft wire hook being pulled from their throat, although matchmen may like to think they do.

Cutting the line and leaving the hook in is not as efficient in terms of fish survival as used to be thought. Small hooks offer a better survival rate, but the best policy is to eat any legal fish that will not survive being unhooked and returned.

If you are taking fish to eat, or for the bait freezer, there are several ways to preserve their quality, especially when they are caught early in a session on a summer's day. Gutting the fish prevents the stomach liquids turning the flesh soft, as does keeping fish separate from one another – lay them out in a covered cool box, bag or fish box. Covering them with beach sand is better than cramming them into a plastic bag and leaving them in the sun. Gutting and filleting your catch means you do not have to dispose of the unwanted, smelly carcass at home – instead, feed it to the crabs or gulls.

"Good fish welfare involves the careful unhooking, handling and release of each fish in as short a time as possible"

Landing large fish from the beach is possible using the waves if it's relatively calm, but in rough situations nothing beats a sharp gaff to snatch a big fish safely from the surf. Some might say this is barbaric and unnecessary, and that would indeed be the case if you wished to return the fish alive. However, attempting to net a fish with a hand-held landing net in a rough sea is dangerous.

From a high pier or rock mark a drop net is the favoured means of landing big fish. A few rules help to ensure that fish are netted efficiently and safely, and the first is always to manoeuvre the fish to the net, not the other way round. Take your time and beware of spare hooks or grip wires. These can easily become entangled in the mesh, and the fish is then trapped outside the net.

Net Tip: In a very strong tide a round net can easily be swept along a pier wall. A square or rectangular-shaped net is far more efficient for walled piers. Don't forget to add a heavy weight to help keep your net in position.

"A drop net is the favoured method of landing a fish from a high pier or rock mark"

THE BAIT COLLECTOR'S CODE

It's essential when bait digging or crab-bing that you replace rocks as you find them and backfill your digging excava-tions as your go. Replacing rocks means that the next crabber may find a crab, whilst leaving rocks upturned kills other marine live dependant on it.

Tidy bait digging is essential to the safety of other shore users, do not dig near to boat moorings, slipways or anywhere that someone might fall or get stuck in your muddy excavation.

Be aware that the crabs and some shell-fish are included in DEFRA's minimum legal sizes and although the majority of local Sea Fishery Committees turn a blind eye to anglers taking undersized crabs as bait, selling them IS illegal.

"Mostly common sense, the bait diggers code not only involves safety but ensures continued bait supplies"

PROTECTED SPECIES

There are several rare or threatened species that are protected by law, meaning it's illegal to capture them. You are advised to release any of these you hook accidentally as soon as possible.

The Allis Shad and the Sturgeon are two that are found in salt water.
Others are freshwater species: burbot, powan and vendace.

The Twaite shad is not a protected species although many of the angling organisations and clubs ban these from competitions and specimen events because of the confusion of identity between the two shads.

"If you catch a rare species it's advised to release it as soon as possible"

The right of the common man to fish from the sea shore is written into Magna Carta, and you can fish almost anywhere around the coast of the UK. The only exceptions are Ministry of Defence land, including firing ranges, and regions of land where rights to the shore-line were given away before the Magna Carta. In many cases it is access to the sea shore that can prove a problem, whereas the strip of land between the mean low tide and mean high tide is Crown Land, and from that you can fish. The angler has more rights in respect of fishing than many other members of the public, including those who play ball games or walk their dogs.

However, while the right to fish has not been changed since Magna Carta, modern angling for sport is different from the original intention and may yet be tested in a court of law. Under the existing law it needs an Act of Parliament to stop angling on Crown Land – local councils cannot take away your right to fish. Bait digging, being a part of fishing, is also protected by the law to some extent, although only in terms of personal bait digging – digging commercially is not included. In all cases anglers must give way to boats. Some boat owners are not aware of the distances today's anglers can cast, but there is no excuse for casting towards or near a boat.

Fishing in a crowd, the banter and the cama-raderie are what many anglers enjoy, but even when fishing among friends there are some basic rules to observe. Always give other anglers plenty of room, especially if they were on site before you.

"Disputes involving crossed lines and tangles can be avoided... look before you cast"

ishing spots are always first-come,
irst-served. Don't muscle in on others, or
eserve places for mates who have not
rrived, or take up more than your share
f room with your tackle. Keep terminal
igs and tackle, especially rigs and hooks,
idy and out of the way of passers by.

f you are a novice pier angler, pay atten-
ion to the tactics of the seasoned pier
nglers. Many of them will be only too
villing to offer advice and encourage-
nent.

asting is a major danger, and it is impor-
ant to use common sense.
 crowded venue, especially a pier, is not
he place for a full pendulum or danger-
us power casting styles.
lso ensure that the tackle you use is safe,
nd includes a casting shock leader,

even for the overhead thump when using
leads of 4oz-plus. Look before you cast
and remember, non-anglers are not
always aware of the dangers!

Casting tangles are best sorted before
they happen, so keep an eye on your lines
and those of others. If they cross, uncross
them before the problem magnifies!

Respect the venue. Do not cut bait on pier
seats, damage life-saving equipment or
abuse the pier furniture. Do not urinate
on (or off) the pier!

Do not stand on pier walls – it's a bad
example to young anglers, and dangerous.

Litter is a modern problem and it does
seem that many, including anglers, see
nothing wrong with discarding what they
don't want. Check a Premiership football
ground on a Saturday and it will be far
worse than any beach. However, leaving
litter cannot be excused, and most clubs
and organisations have now imposed the
threat of a ban on competitors in competitions who leave bait papers, plastic bags
and the like on the beach. Freelance
anglers, especially the less serious, seem to
be to blame for the majority of the litter,
although let's not forget the flotsam. I
would urge all anglers to include a plastic
rubbish sack in their tackle box and use it
to remove any rubbish on the beach.

A word about discarded terminal rigs.
It's not always a good idea to dump your
baited rigs in the rubbish bin, because
these might end up on the rubbish tip
where they can be picked up by birds.
It is best to remove bait from hooks and
then wrap rig line around your hand and
cut it into small lengths before putting it
in the rubbish. Similarly, any large amount
of mono line should be cut into small,
less dangerous, lengths or burnt
before disposal.

LUCK

I have included a section on luck in this book because it is something no angler can control or avoid, and we all have to live with the consequences. Some say you make your own luck – I say confidence can make a difference to the individual's luck, but bad luck always comes to an end sooner or later. Unfortunately, the same can be said of the other kind!

Being positive and not giving up easily will affect your results, and being around when your luck comes back is a reason to always carry on when all around you is falling apart. That's not to say I have never given up and gone home prematurely, but on occasions I have caught a bonus fish on my last cast or when my confidence has been at an extremely low ebb.

You will know when the gods are against you – some call it Murphy's or Sods Law. That's when all fails, your angling world crumbles, everything goes wrong and it is probably best to cut your losses and go home, driving carefully.

Equally, on some days all goes perfectly. Red-letter days are to be savoured, remembered, retold and embellished over a pint. They are the ultimate angling memory most of us cling to – we are less likely to remember the bad days.

But overall, every day we fish brings renewed hope, enthusiasm and a clean sheet, which is why angling is so much fun. You just never know what Lady Luck has in store for you!

ANGLING CLUBS

The local angling club is the backbone of sea angling, and around the UK there are thousands of small clubs based around a town, pier, working men's club or pub. I am a staunch supporter of organised angling, and have been a member of a club since I was a junior. The club brings not only a social side to the sport, but a really effective schooling and coaching system for seniors and juniors alike to learn the skills that make them better anglers.

Local knowledge is a major factor in sea angling success, and while many anglers look for a single factor to improve their performance – be it tackle, bait, casting or rigs – the truth is that a combination of things is most often the key to consistent results. The angling club provides not only a way to learn the basic sea angling skills, but that essential local knowledge often essential to get the best from a venue.

You can join most sea angling clubs for less than £10. They generally use local venues for regular club fishing competitions, and these are a very effective and quick way for the novice angler to learn a combination of skills
– if you are struggling, seek out the club champion. He is very often the man to watch.

Most clubs are affiliated to a larger organisation, and in the UK the National Federation of Sea Anglers (NFSA) is the largest. Wales (WFSA), Scotland (SFSA) and Ireland (IFSA) also have national bodies. There are a number of specialist clubs for species (National Mullet Club, Conger Club, Bass Anglers) as well as organisations that specialise in overseas internationals (EFSA – European Federation of Sea Anglers and SAMF – Sea Anglers Match Federation).

HOW TO RUN A CLUB MATCH

Are you thinking of entering a club fishing competition, or are you a club secretary who wants to start organising events? Here are the basics of organising club matches.

A major problem for sea angling competition organisers is that only one angler can win an event, the rest are runners-up. Regular winners are the death knell of many a club and in recent times the introduction of cash prizes and the growth in the professionalism of anglers has resulted in a decline in competition entries. However, not all clubs allow a few individual anglers to dominate their events by catering for a range of angling abilities and promoting the luck element of sea angling.

As a lifetime match angler of some ability I am sorry to say that the likes of me can ruin a club match series, indeed, I and plenty of others have been refused membership for winning too often. However, matchmen and novice can fish together in a club if the format of events is managed to cater for both levels.
First priority for the organiser is setting the entry fee, serious matchmen want big cash prizes, novices a chance of winning and the most successful format is a small entry fee of between £1 and £3, including an optional pool. Offering small, non cash prizes or trophies only deters the more mercenary match anglers and competitions based around biggest fish of species as well as aggregate weight help promote a wider range of winners. It's my belief that many clubs have gone OTT adopting open competition formats, especially cash prizes, to the detriment of their club events.

Fishing at club level allows a greater degree of freedom from rules. Rover events where competitors can fish where they like and in groups of friends within a small boundary are popular. These trust anglers to be honest and this fosters a better social atmosphere, secrecy yes, but with a grin! Pegged events are more secure from the likely cheat, but allow the better anglers to dominate. Chose your format carefully - lots of clubs mix and match rovers, zoned and pegged events as well as different venues.

Short evening competitions arranged between 7pm and 10pm are the basis of many club's existence, their finances too. Members meet at a central point, like a tackle shop, pub, club house if they have one, then leave at a set time, fish and return for the weigh in inside a time limit. Plenty of scope for catch, measure, weigh and release points for species or weight, whilst fishing rules can be arranged and adjusted to suit competitors, venue, time of year etc. It's social fishing, still plenty of competition, but with less of an edge than a large open event.

A word about selecting fixtures: most clubs fish fortnightly to suit tide times, but ensure that the most productive season, fishing times and venues are selected, anglers catching fish are far happier than those blanking.
Standard competition rules include the use of one rod only with a maximum of three hooks. Some clubs permit the use of baits like lugworm and squid only, others raise the size minimum limits of the more common species. Pairs, mixed pairs, teams, juniors, ladies and species events also help to spread the involvement and potential success to all competitors and some clubs even operate a handicap system or divisions to split the range of angling abilities.

"Angling clubs bring a great social side to sea fishing, as well as a regular chance to fish competitions"

CLUB COMPETITIONS

These are most often fished on a weekday night or a weekend day over a set time at a specified venue. Clubs usually choose the most favourable tides for competitions, and as these occur every fortnight clubs – on average – hold two a month, plus the odd weekend event. Competitions are usually organised around a rover format, whereby competitors can fish anywhere within a set boundary – or (favourite on piers) they are pegged, with the competitors drawing for positions.

The winner is decided by a variety of methods, with the heaviest catch (bag weight) the most commonly used.

Biggest fish, most fish, most species and best specimen are also used at times to determine the winner, and these categories are generally favoured to spread the prizes as well.

Many clubs run a seasonal series of events, with the annual prize-giving being one of the most important social occasions of the year.

Odd, isn't it, how freelance-caught fish are always far bigger than those caught in competitions? Obviously proof that freelance catches are always exaggerated somewhat, and that it does pay to ignore some of the tackle shop rumours and instead look at club match results. This will give the truest picture of what is being caught from various venues.

COMPETITION RULES

The basic competition fishing rule is one rod with a maximum of three hooks. Spare rods are allowed without a terminal rig attached, while spare terminal rigs can be ready-baited.

Individual clubs and organisations have variations on these rules, such as two rods being allowed with a maximum of three hooks between them. A treble hook is usually viewed as three hooks, so it's always worth checking with competition organisers, especially if you are considering using a lure with multi-trebles.

Other rules concern the fishing times, the start and finish and the time given to return fish for weighing in.

Some events have local fishing rules, such as a ban on a particular part of a venue, or strict boundaries within which competitors may fish.

Some have bait restrictions, hook size limits or a ban on certain species. In all cases it makes sound sense to study the rules carefully before fishing. If you're not sure about any aspect of the competition, ask someone who does know. It's no good being wise after the event and pleading ignorance – you'll still be disqualified!

Chapter 8 **Safety, Conservation and Rules** *Competitions*

Catch, measure and release competitions have increased in numbers in recent years, although in many cases for the wrong reasons. I was one of the first to introduce catch and release via the Sea Anglers Match Federation formed by myself and Clive Richards in 1979, but the adoption of reduced size limits, even no size limit at all, catches the smallest of fish. This is not necessary from many venues and has alienated lots of regular

anglers from match fishing and made match fishing too élitist in some cases.
A major problem with catch and release events using no minimum size is that competitors adopt the use of smaller and smaller hook sizes.

These catch the smaller fish which would otherwise not be caught under standard size limits

and are therefore self-defeating in terms of conservation. Any event fished on a catch and release basis needs a 'size 2 hook minimum' rule to prevent the slaughter of the tiny fish.

At club level, keeping the standard size limit minimums and returning fish is popular, especially for the species that few anglers eat – fish such as smoothhound, mullet and dogfish. The effect on localised stocks is noticeable.

If fish are being weighed in after the end of the competition, they are measured before weighing. The measuring is from nose to tail, on a proper fish measure available from most tackle dealers. Clubs and organisers can set their own minimums and many do, slightly above the legal limit or bigger.

In catch, measure and return events the angler's catch is recorded on a bag label. Most popular is one point for each centimetre of fish length. However, this does favour the smaller fish, so many clubs award bonus points for the bigger fish. Weight-for-length charts are also popular. In other events, fish under a certain size are returned, but count for a particular score. A combination score based around points and species can also be used.

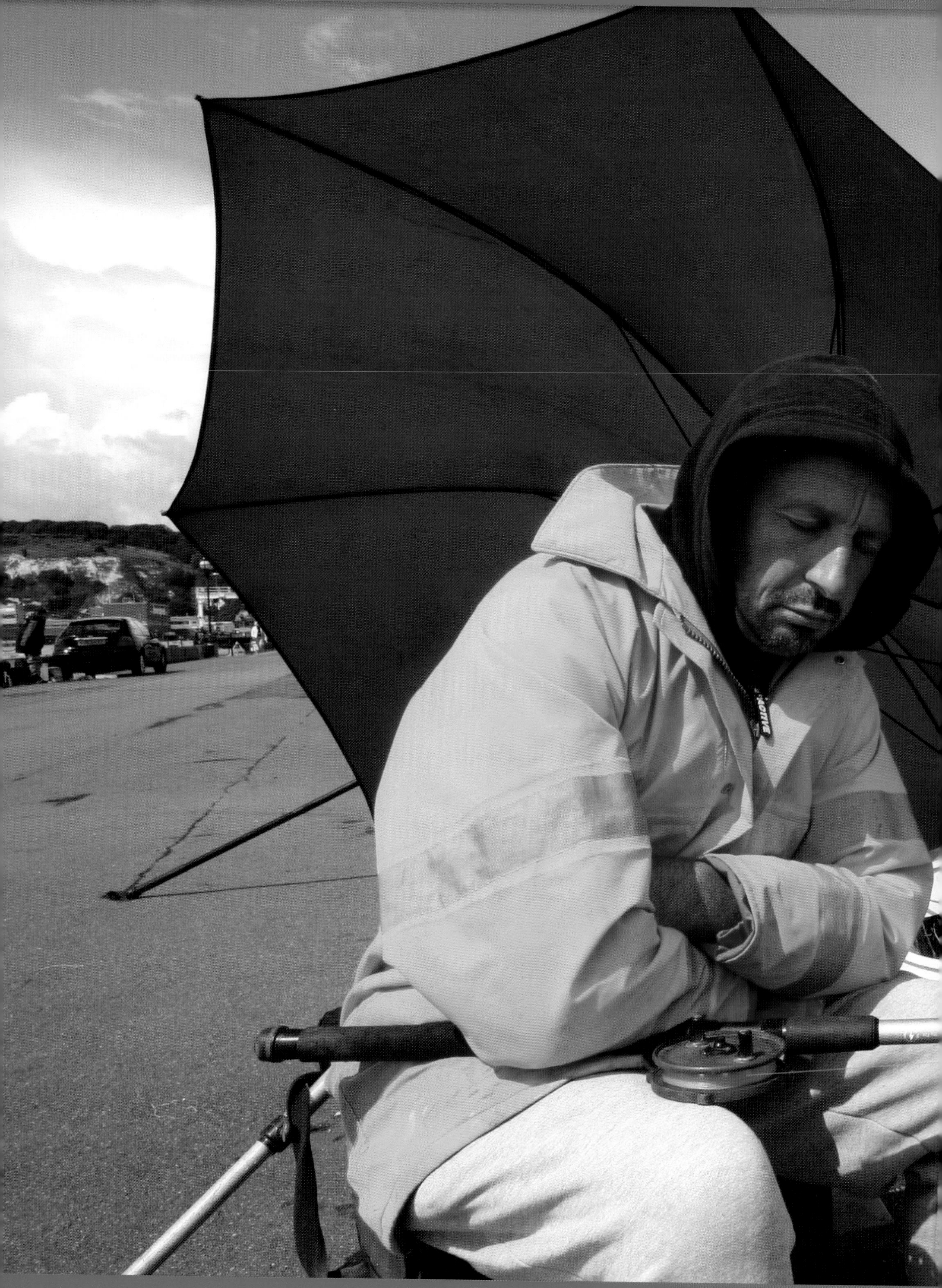

I have been a sea angler for more years than I want to admit, but every day I learn something new. If I had to give the sea angler one vital piece of advice, it would be never to think that you know it all, or that you have found the perfect solution to catching fish. So many anglers become totally set in their ways and approach to angling. Many even ignore the changes in seasons and fish behaviour, and the advancements in tackle and tactics. A majority do not bother to keep a note of past results, and so many fish just the one method or like robots, no matter where they are. Keeping an open mind to progress, and remembering as much as possible of my past experiences, has kept me successful over the years. However, although sea angling can be an extremely intense sport it can also be simply a way to pass your leisure time – it's up to you. A novice can beat a world champion and age is not a barrier to success. You can fish at your pace and even enjoy it in your sleep (just like this angler)!

T.

U.

W.